OZ CLARKE'S
WINE COMPANION

BORDEAUX

GUIDE

JAMES LAWTHER MW

De Agostini *Editions*

HOW TO USE THIS BOOK

MAPS

For further information on the wine regions see the Fold-out Map.

Each tour in the book has a map to accompany it. These are not detailed road maps; readers are advised to buy such maps to avoid local navigation difficulties.

▬▬▬	Motorway (*Autoroute*)
▬▬▬	Major road
▬▬▬	Minor road
▬▬▬	Other road
◆	Wine property

FACT FILES

Each tour has an accompanying fact file, which lists sources of information on the region, markets and festivals, and where to buy wine. There is also a short listing of hotels and restaurants.

Ⓗ Hotel
Ⓡ Restaurant

To give an indication of prices, we have used a simple rating system.

Ⓕ Inexpensive
ⒻⒻ Moderate
ⒻⒻⒻ Expensive

WINE PRODUCERS

Producers' names in small capitals refer to entries in the A–Z on page 70.

Visiting arrangements
✓ Visitors welcome
⊘ By appointment
✗ No visitors

Wine styles made
🍷 Red
🍷 White
🍷 Rosé

Please note that guidebook information is inevitably subject to change. We suggest that, wherever possible, you telephone in advance to check addresses, opening times, etc.

While every care has been taken in preparing this guide, the publishers cannot accept any liability for any consequence arising from the use of information contained in it.

First published
by De Agostini Editions
Interpark House
7 Down Street
London W1Y 7DS

Distributed in the U.S.
by Stewart, Tabori & Chang,
a division of US Media
Holdings Inc
575 Broadway
New York NY10012

Distributed in Canada
by General Publishing
Company Ltd
30 Lesmill Road, Don Mills
Ontario M3B 2T6

Oz Clarke's Wine Companion:
Bordeaux
copyright © 1997 Websters
International Publishers

Fold-out Map
copyright © 1997 Websters
International Publishers
Text copyright © 1997
Oz Clarke
Maps copyright © 1997
Websters International Publishers
Some maps and text have been
adapted from *Oz Clarke's Wine
Atlas* copyright © 1995 Websters
International Publishers

Guide
copyright © 1997 Websters
International Publishers

Created and designed by Websters
International Publishers Ltd
Axe & Bottle Court
70 Newcomen Street
London SE1 1YT

UK ISBN: 1 86212 032 3
A CIP catalogue record for this book is available from the British Library.

US ISBN: 1 86212 036 6
Library of Congress Catalog
Card Number 97–065430

OZ CLARKE
Oz Clarke is one of the world's leading wine experts, with a formidable reputation based on his extensive wine knowledge and accessible, no-nonsense approach. He appears regularly on BBC Television and has won all the major wine-writing awards in the USA and UK. His bestselling titles include *Oz Clarke's Wine Atlas*, *Oz Clarke's Pocket Wine Guide* and the *Microsoft Wine Guide* CD-ROM.

JAMES LAWTHER MW
Master of Wine, James Lawther lives in Bordeaux where he often leads wine tours. He writes on wine for numerous international publications.

Associate Editorial Director
Fiona Holman
Associate Art Director
Nigel O'Gorman
Editor
Pauline Savage
Art Editor
Christopher Howson
Sub-editor
Gwen Rigby
Editorial Assistant
Emma Richards
Wine Consultant
Phillip Williamson
DTP
Jonathan Harley
Index
Naomi Good
Editorial Director
Claire Harcup
Pictorial Cartography
Keith and Sue Gage,
Contour Designs
Pictorial Map Editor
Wink Lorch
Touring Maps
European Map Graphics

Colour separations by Columbia
Offset, Singapore
Printed in Hong Kong

Photographs:
Front cover Château Cantemerle is a top producer in the Haut-Médoc AC.
Page 1 Ch. d'Yquem is the producer of the world's best sweet wine.
Page 3 Cabernet Sauvignon is one of Bordeaux's great grape varieties.

Contents

Introduction

The world's greatest treasures, its most enduring pleasures, aren't always the easiest to understand. Subtlety and nuance need to be studied before their thrilling complexity begins to fascinate the mind and grip the soul. Only then, when you have committed yourself, are the glories revealed. And nowhere is this more true than in Bordeaux.

With the exception of a few sheltered slopes around St-Émilion, most of Bordeaux's best vineyards seem relatively flat and formless. Apart from some glorious vine-packed forest glades in Pessac-Léognan, most of Bordeaux's best wines come from broad, open spaces. And on your first day in the region, it is easy to wonder what all the fuss is about.

But the area will grow on you, just as it did on me. From my very first visit, I became fascinated with the slight variations between the vineyards of St-Julien and Pauillac; St-Émilion and Pomerol; Sauternes and Barsac. And as you get to know the different villages and vineyards, their different soils, and their different aspect to the sun and protection from the wind and rain, the remarkable range of wines that Bordeaux produces will begin to make sense.

Bordeaux's red wines have, for two centuries or more, been regarded as the classics to which winemakers throughout the world aspire. This is due not only to their wonderful power, resolute, sometimes austere, sometimes fleshy, perfumed with cedar, blackcurrant, chocolate or plums, but also to their ability to age. The leading properties generally make substantial volumes of a single wine. This has meant that connoisseurs around the world could build collections of many vintages, and as they shared their bottles with others, the reputation of the top properties grew. Although the Pessac-Léognan vineyards were the first to become famous, the wines that have led the charge in modern times have been those of the top Haut-Médoc communes and the plumper, more sensuous wines of St-Émilion and Pomerol.

Even so, the sweet wines of Sauternes, and the dry whites of Pessac-Léognan and Graves are frequently of similar quality. Yet these great wines make up only a small percentage of Bordeaux's production. The majority of its wines are lighter, simpler, more affordable styles, but Bordeaux's brilliance lies in the fact that it offers a stairway, in both reds and whites, from the simple wines to the majestic, complex and expensive wines at the pinnacle, and as you work your way up, a thread of character, based on the grape varieties, but above all, on the place they are grown, still links the pauper to the prince.

Oz Clarke

Although Bordeaux is by no means the world's most beautiful wine region, it won't take you long to become mesmerized by the parade of châteaux, both great and small.

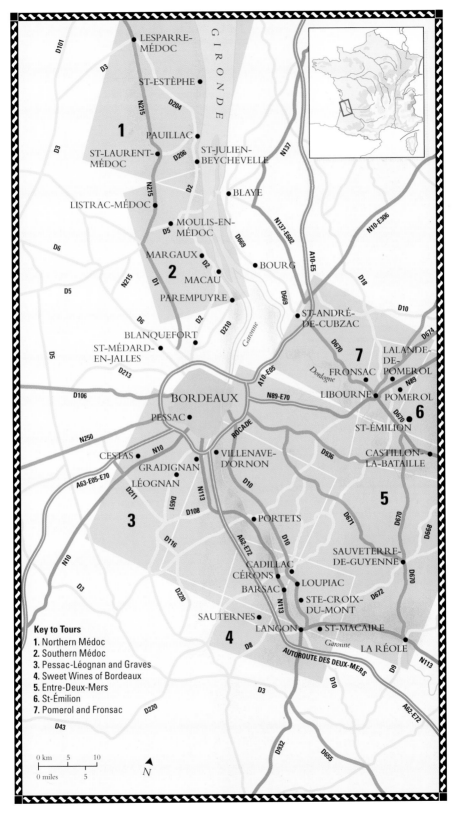

LESPARRE-
MÉDOC

G I R O N D E

ST-ESTÈPHE

D204

N215

D3

1

PAUILLAC

ST-JULIEN-
BEYCHEVELLE

ST-LAURENT-
MÉDOC

D206

N137

D3

N215

BLAYE

LISTRAC-MÉDOC

N137-E602

D6

MOULIS-EN-
MÉDOC

D5

D669

N10-E306

MARGAUX

D2

BOURG

A10-E5

D18

2

MACAU

N215

D1

D5

PAREMPUYRE

D669

D10

ST-ANDRÉ-
DE-CUBZAC

D674

D6

D2

D210

Garonne

D670

BLANQUEFORT

D5

ST-MÉDARD-
EN-JALLES

7

LALANDE-
DE-
POMEROL

D213

Dordogne

FRONSAC

D106

BORDEAUX

N89-E70

LIBOURNE

POMEROL

A10-E05

N250

PESSAC

ROCADE

6

ST-ÉMILION

D670

CESTAS

N10

VILLENAVE-
D'ORNON

D936

CASTILLON-
LA-BATAILLE

A63-E05-E70

GRADIGNAN

D211

LÉOGNAN

D651

N113

D10

5

D671

D670

D116

D108

3

PORTETS

D10

D668

SAUVETERRE-
DE-GUYENNE

N10

A62-E72

CADILLAC

CÉRONS

D3

BARSAC

LOUPIAC

D672

D670

D220

STE-CROIX-
DU-MONT

SAUTERNES

N113

Key to Tours
1. Northern Médoc
2. Southern Médoc
3. Pessac-Léognan and Graves
4. Sweet Wines of Bordeaux
5. Entre-Deux-Mers
6. St-Émilion
7. Pomerol and Fronsac

4

LANGON

ST-MACAIRE

Garonne

LA RÉOLE

N113

AUTOROUTE DES DEUX-MERS

D8

D9

A62-E72

D220

D3

D10

D43

0 km   5   10

0 miles   5

N

D332

D655

This inky-black top St-Julien will slowly turn ruby, then garnet and finally brickish with maturity. Pale-coloured Bordeaux Blanc will become a deeper yellow-gold with age.

Wine at a Glance

Bordeaux is the largest fine wine region in the world. While the prestigious châteaux represent no more than 5% of the total number, they account for perhaps 95% of Bordeaux's reputation. Such is the influence of the region as a whole that vintage assessments of its red wines, or claret, still dominate the perception of vintages elsewhere – for many wine drinkers a year has a truly special ring to it only when it is a great success in Bordeaux.

Grape Varieties

Bordeaux's red grapes are responsible for the most frequently copied wine style in the world. The white grapes are more vulnerable to the vagaries of Bordeaux's fickle weather but are capable of no less greatness.

Cabernet Sauvignon
The Médoc, with its signature grape, Cabernet Sauvignon, has made Bordeaux the inspiration and reference point for the world's winemakers. The grape provides deep colour, ample body, abundant fruit and good levels of tannin and acidity. Made with sufficient concentration and structure, it ages impressively, particularly in oak, adding further complexity but retaining finesse. The best have intense blackcurrant fruit and lead pencil flavours with cigar box aroma, becoming rich and cedary or minerally and herbal with age.

Cabernet Sauvignon

Merlot
Merlot is far more widely planted than Cabernet Sauvignon, prefers a cooler clay soil, and is earlier ripening but more susceptible to disease. It produces wines with less tannin and acidity than its rival, resulting in softer, rounder wines that are more accessible when young but have less aging potential. Merlot is most successful with Cabernets Sauvignon

Merlot

and Franc, when it can reveal a berry, plummy, fruitcake flavour or a darker black cherry character.

Cabernet Franc
This variety is always blended, usually with Cabernet Sauvignon and Merlot. The wines are softer, with less colour and tannin but more aroma, and have a pronounced herbal and floral character.

Sémillon
Sémillon is the mainstay of Bordeaux's sweet wines because of its susceptibility to the fungus Botrytis cinerea, or noble rot. Fine

Sémillon

Sauternes can taste of ripe citrus fruits or peach, honey, spice and marmalade. In a dry white blend it can be ripe, tropical fruited and aromatic.

Sauvignon Blanc
In Bordeaux Sauvignon Blanc is often blended with Sémillon, resulting in a range of vibrant flavours and styles. The wines are full, ripe and round; skin contact prior to fermentation and the use of new oak add further complexity and improve structure and aging potential. The result is a creamy richness with melon, ripe peach and exotic notes added to a grapefruit and floral character.

Sauvignon Blanc

Other Varieties
Petit Verdot and Malbec (or Pressac) are very minor members of the so-called Bordeaux five, the former limited to the best properties of the Médoc. Other lesser white grapes include Colombard, Ugni Blanc and Muscadelle (for cheaper sweet wines), but all three are in decline.

Understanding Red and Dry White Bordeaux

You can learn something about a wine simply by looking at the bottle – the traditional shape and colour of a Bordeaux bottle are found around the world.

Until recently, lead capsules were common, especially for Cru Classé Bordeaux, but EU regulations now require capsules to be made from tin foil or plastic.

The classic Bordeaux bottle is high shouldered and has been copied throughout the world for Cabernet- or Merlot-based wines. Producers of New World Sauvignon Blanc that owes more to Bordeaux than the Loire in style may be more inclined to choose this shape too.

Vieilles Vignes, or old vines, usually denotes the most prestigious selection of grapes, whatever the age of the vines.

The generic AC for dry white Bordeaux.

The indentation, or punt, in the bottom of the bottle is said to increase strength, but in reality simply makes a useful thumb-hold for a sommelier.

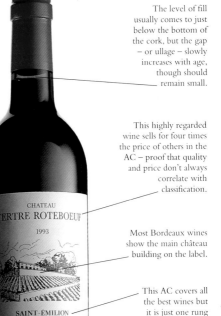

The level of fill usually comes to just below the bottom of the cork, but the gap – or ullage – slowly increases with age, though should remain small.

This highly regarded wine sells for four times the price of others in the AC – proof that quality and price don't always correlate with classification.

Most Bordeaux wines show the main château building on the label.

This AC covers all the best wines but it is just one rung above the most basic category.

Bordeaux bottles are usually made from olive-green glass. The heavier and darker the bottle, the greater the protection from light and heat.

WINE CLASSIFICATIONS

The French system of *appellation contrôlée* (AC) applies to Bordeaux at 4 levels:
• The general Bordeaux AC for red, white and rosé. Wines with a higher minimum alcohol level can use Bordeaux Supérieur AC.
• More specific regional ACs, such as Médoc and Entre-Deux-Mers.
• Village ACs that comprise no more than a few communes and include world-famous names such as Margaux and St-Julien.
• Crémant de Bordeaux, for Champagne-method sparkling wines. In addition, wines are classified according to historical precepts:

The 1855 Classification
Based on a commercial assessment by brokers of the day (supplemented by a blind tasting), it was intended purely as a guide to the wines

entered in the Great Paris Exhibition in 1855. There are 5 Crus or categories (from Premier down to Cinquième) but only first and second are recognized by the EU labelling laws. The only change has been the promotion of Ch. Mouton-Rothschild to Premier Cru in 1973.

1855 Classification of Sauternes
Sauternes and Barsac were also included in the 1855 Classification, with 2 main categories, Premier Cru and Deuxième Cru, and a separate level, Premier Cru Supérieur, for Ch. d'Yquem.

Cru Bourgeois
Originally classified in 1932 and revised in 1969 and 1984, non-Cru Classé Médoc and Haut-Médoc properties are grouped into 3 categories: Cru Bourgeois Exceptionnel, Cru Grand Bourgeois and simple Cru Bourgeois. However,

laws permit the use only of Cru Bourgeois on the label.

Graves
Ch. Haut-Brion was the only Graves property included in the 1855 Classification. Subsequently a single-class alphabetical list of red wines was issued in 1953 and of whites in 1959. AC laws now differentiate between Graves and the northern part of Pessac-Léognan.

1996 St-Émilion
First drawn up in 1955, and revised in 1985 and 1996. Of the 4 levels, the most basic is St-Émilion AC. The next, St-Émilion Grand Cru AC, covers hundreds of wines; within this there are 2 categories, Grand Cru Classé, (55 châteaux) and Premier Grand Cru Classé, made up of 13 properties: Ausone and Cheval-Blanc have the suffix A, the other 11 B. There is no classification for Pomerol.

THE CHÂTEAU SYSTEM

The château is the concept upon which the whole of Bordeaux's wine is based. French for 'castle', a château is not always the grandiose building it sounds. In fact, in the 18th and 19th centuries, wealthy landowners started a trend in adding rather incongruous, fanciful edifices to their humbler estate buildings, to the point where virtually all wine-making properties assumed the title of château. In wine terms, all 'château' means is a vine-growing, wine-making estate.

Despite the image of a château surrounded by its vineyards, many properties now own hectares of vines that are scattered about the surrounding countryside. The Bordeaux classification system (see page 7), however, is historically linked to the individual properties, not to the vineyards themselves, and so takes no account of the change of ownership of land over the years. In fact, the wines today may be made from almost entirely different plots of vines from those originally assessed.

How to Choose Bordeaux

Some knowledge of ACs is useful for gaining an idea of the style of Bordeaux you might want to drink, but the château name is all-important, even with an inexpensive Bordeaux AC. Choose a good but not too fashionable name from a lesser year and it will probably be better and cheaper than a better-known château producing mediocre wines in a good vintage. The year is useful in deciding when to drink the wine, i.e. whether it is immediately approachable or for cellaring.

Though a Cinquième Cru, the label indicates only Grand Cru Classé and not the château's specific level.

This relatively obscure château has a modest reputation and price, but its most recent vintages offer the greatest richness.

12.5% alcohol by volume is typical in Bordeaux red wines. Too much or too little makes the wine unbalanced.

Pauillac is one of the most famous village ACs in the world.

This proprietor owns only one other château. Large corporations may own several properties.

While 1990 is considered the greatest vintage of the past decade, investment and wine-making expertise have eliminated so-called bad vintages.

GLOSSARY

Barrique The Bordeaux barrel of 225 litres, made from OAK.

Botrytis cinerea Fungus responsible for NOBLE ROT and GREY ROT.

Claret English term for red Bordeaux wine.

Clairet The name from which claret is derived now refers to a lighter-style red wine.

Chai Cellar, often underground, where the wine is matured (in BARRIQUES) following vinification.

Château Wine estate, or the main buildings located on it.

Commune Village and its surrounding area – the smallest political division.

Cru Classé Classed Growths (see Classifications p.7).

Égrappage French for destalking.

Élevage Handling and maturing of the wine after fermentation and before bottling.

En Primeur/Futures Sale of part of the most recent vintage usually 1–2 years before it is bottled and shipped.

Extract Soluble substances in wine that influence structure and flavour.

Fermentation (alcoholic) Conversion of grape sugar into alcohol and carbon dioxide with the aid of yeasts.

Filtration Removal of solids and impurities from wine before bottling. The implication for quality and stability is currently one of the most contentious issues in wine production.

Fining Clarifying wine by the addition of a coagulant such as egg whites to remove soluble particles. Part of the same debate as FILTRATION.

Generic Without further qualification or classification – in Bordeaux, the basic category within which a wine falls.

Grey Rot Results from the fungus BOTYTRIS CINEREA in damp and cold conditions, bringing unwanted flavours to wine.

Mesoclimate/Microclimate Correctly used, mesoclimate refers to the climate of a distinct geographical area, microclimate to conditions surrounding the vine itself.

Must Mulch of grape juice, skins, pulp and pips.

Noble Rot or Pourriture Noble Results from the benevolent action of the fungus BOTRYTIS CINEREA – shrivelling the grape and intensifying the sugar. Particularly successful in Sauternes when hot, humid mornings are followed by hot, dry afternoons.

Oak Wood used for BARRIQUES for the maturation of red wines and the fermentation and aging of sweet white wines.

Organic Viticulture Avoidance of chemical fertilizers, herbicides and pesticides in the vineyard. Organic wine-making does not use certain additives.

Petit Château Unclassified property that produces basic Bordeaux red and white wines.

Racking Periodic clarification and aeration of a wine as a part of its ÉLEVAGE. The wine is run out of the

barrel to allow the removal of the fine sediment (lees).

Residual Sugar Unfermented sugar left at the end of FERMENTATION, which determines the degree of sweetness of the wine.

Remontage Pumping the juice over the skins in red wine FERMENTATION, typically twice a day. Improves aeration and extraction.

Rosé Pink wine usually produced by running the juice off the skins 24–36 hours after the start of FERMENTATION.

Second Wine A château's secondary offering, made from younger vines or a certain parcel of vineyards. It is usually lighter and more forward, but helps to maintain the quality and consistency of the 'château' wine. It also brings a quicker financial return when there is no EN PRIMEUR market.

Tannin Substance derived from grape skins, stems and pips as well as oak barrels; important to wine structure and aging potential. Its quantity and quality determine the sensation in the mouth.

Terroir Unique physical environment of a vineyard, comprising the soil, elevation, orientation and climate.

Tri Pass made through the vineyard to select grapes affected by NOBLE ROT in the production of Sauternes and other sweet wines.

Yield (rendement) Quantity of grapes or wine produced; usually expressed in hectolitres per hectare.

Understanding Bordeaux Sweet White Wines

Sweetness allied to lusciousness, concentration and power, as well as almost unlimited aging potential, sets the finest Sauternes apart from other sweet wines.

When lying in a wine rack only the neck will be visible, so the marking of the coat of arms and the owner's name make for easier identification.

A specially designed glass for maximum appreciation of high-quality Sauternes – the Riedel Sommelier's Sauternes.

The clear bottle is traditional for sweet white Bordeaux. It shows off the colour of the wine so effectively that it is used by many other producers of sweet wines, even though it provides less protection against light and heat.

A classic Bordeaux label design, with the château building framed by its entrance gate.

750ml and 375ml are common for sweet white Bordeaux, but a thin, elegant 500ml bottle – just the right amount for two – is becoming more popular.

Noble Rot

The five communes of Sauternes and Barsac share a special mesoclimate that enables them to produce their famous sweet wines. Warm, mist-shrouded mornings followed by hot, dry afternoons provide ideal conditions for the fungus *Botrytis cinerea* to grow. Botrytis attacks healthy white grapes, causing them to dehydrate and turn golden, then pink or purple and finally brown, shrivelling them to the size of a raisin. This condition, known as noble rot, has the effect of concentrating the sugars in the grape, enabling the production of intensely sweet wines.

Flavours include ripest peach or nectarine, apricot, honey, marmalade and butterscotch, while some Barsac can add minerally elegance. Not all sweet wines are botrytized, but the occurrence of noble rot is the defining factor of a great sweet wine vintage.

VINTAGES

Traditional Bordeaux wines benefit the most from aging; new-style wines – lush and upfront – are almost instantly drinkable.

1996 Promises to be even better than 95 in the Médoc. More variable elsewhere, but some excellent dry and sweet whites are anticipated.

1995 St-Julien, Pauillac and Pomerol were the most successful, but there are very good wines wherever high levels of tannin are matched by an impressive concentration of fruit. Dry whites are often very good, but only some good Sauternes.

1994 Generally less good than 95, but more concentrated and with riper fruit than the 93s. Best in Pomerol, St-Julien and St-Estèphe. Excellent dry whites, but only some quality sweet white wines.

1993 Rain just before and during the harvest put paid to potentially excellent quality. Good Merlot-based wines from St-Émilion and Pomerol.

1992 A poor year of light wines.

1991 Stick to top names in the Graves and Médoc.

1990 Extremely hot but great year, probably the best and most consistent of the golden trio of 1988–90. Sauternes is sensational.

1989 Médoc quality is irregular. Excellent St-Émilion and Pomerol. Less consistently great Sauternes.

1988 A classic, slightly more austere vintage than the two that followed. Ageworthy northern Médoc and excellent Graves. Pomerol was more variable. Outstanding Sauternes and some very good dry whites.

1987 A light but stylish vintage – the best names are good now.

1986 St-Julien, Pauillac and St-Estèphe for keeping another 10–15 years. Great Sauternes.

1985 Wonderfully consistent and charming. Drink now or keep.

1984 Tough – in general avoid.

1983 Very good, Margaux and Sauternes excellent.

1982 Outstanding, ripe, rich and consistent. Drink now or keep.

1981 Overlooked but good.

Older vintages 1979 and 1978 are drinking well, though the best of the 78 Médoc will keep; 1976, 75 and 71 are good for Sauternes; 1970 for some lovely reds still capable of further age; 1966 for St-Julien and Pauillac; 1964 for St-Émilion and Pomerol. 1961 is an all-time classic and many properties have not yet bettered their efforts here.

For vintages beyond 1961, only the Premiers Crus can offer something special.

Other good years 1959 55 53 52 49 47 45 34 29 28 26 24 21 20.

A local market in Bordeaux is the best place to buy fresh, seasonal fruit and vegetables. Some markets are now specializing in organically grown produce.

Regional Food

Bordeaux is one of the capitals of French gastronomy, with a regional cuisine that is rich, full and generous in style. Its strength lies in the variety of produce available not only within the region but from the surrounding *départements*. Typical regional dishes include large succulent slabs of *entrecôte* (sirloin steak), Pauillac lamb, duck, Arcachon oysters and lampreys from the Gironde. Add to this red or white wine sauces with marrow 'à la bordelaise' and a little Spanish and Mediterranean influence, with the liberal use of garlic, onions and shallots, and the notion of a cuisine of 'character' begins to take shape.

Regional Produce

The Atlantic Ocean, Gironde estuary and local rivers have long provided a healthy supply of crustaceans, shellfish and sea and river fish. Oysters from the Bassin d'Arcachon, *lamproies* (lampreys) and sturgeon from the Gironde, *alose* (shad) in the spring and small shrimps (*chevrettes*) are just a few of the local specialities.

Beef is a staple, most usually found in restaurants as *côte de boeuf, entrecôte, tournedos* and veal. Beef from Bazas in the south-east of the Gironde is of particular note. Tender Pauillac lamb is milk-fed and raised on the salt-grass pastures of the Médoc. Poultry (duck, chicken and guinea-fowl) and *foie gras* are also traditional to Bordeaux, with the source more than likely from within the *départements* of the Dordogne, Gers or Landes.

When the hunting season opens in September game dishes abound, in particular rabbit, hare and wild duck and the rarer *bécasse* (woodcock) and *palombe* (wood-pigeon). Also available in the autumn is a variety of mushrooms, in particular *cèpes*. Asparagus from Blaye is another seasonal delicacy. Those with a sweet tooth can indulge in St-Émilion macaroons or the *cannelés* from Bordeaux.

There is a wealth of local food markets operating on various days of the week and a variety of regional produce is always available. The Monday market at Castillon-la-Bataille is one of the largest, and in the southern limits of the Entre-Deux-Mers the Saturday market at la Réole on the banks of the Garonne attracts a healthy selection of small, local producers.

In the city of Bordeaux the Marché des Capucins, just off the cours de la Marne, is open daily from midnight to 12.30pm for traders and the public alike. Also open daily in the centre of the city, and now located in a modern glass building, is the Marché des Grands Hommes. There are two open-air markets of note in the old part of the city, the

MATCHING WINE AND FOOD

A whole palette of wine styles is available in Bordeaux (dry, fruity or complex whites; sweet whites; rosés; supple or rich, elegant reds; sparkling wines) so whatever the dish, there should be a wine to match. Bordeaux wines are in essence food wines. The classic red Bordeaux that has a tannic edge is the perfect foil for the region's rich cuisine.

If you are having food cooked with wine, you should ideally drink the same style of wine or a superior version with the meal.

Here are some of the more classic combinations:

Duck or goose liver is traditionally served with a glass of Sauternes (as is Roquefort cheese) – a combination that may sound unlikely until tried.

Crisp white Graves or Entre-Deux-Mers go perfectly with the local oysters and other shellfish.

Meat dishes demand more substantial wines. A Cru Classé Pauillac is the classic partner for roast lamb. The choice for beef is open-ended. *Entrecôte à la bordelaise* can be enjoyed with a Médoc or red Graves, *filet de boeuf* with a Fronsac. Game, too, cries out for the fine reds of the region, preferably with some bottle age for a dish with a pronounced flavour. Try a Pomerol or St-Émilion with duck, partridge or hare.

The lighter sweet wines such as Loupiac and Ste-Croix-du-Mont are delicious served cold with fruit-based desserts.

Cèpe mushrooms are used in a variety of dishes in Bordeaux.

Marché St-Michel, which operates on Saturdays, and the Marché St-Pierre, which functions on Thursdays and sells only organically produced food.

There are limited opportunities for buying at source so for gourmet food stick to the markets or speciality shops in central Bordeaux. Dubernet, in the rue Michel-Montaigne, has an appetizing selection of *foies gras* and game pâtés. A good selection of cheeses can be found at Jean d'Alos in the rue Montesquieu and at Baud et Millet, just off the Place Tourny. For real *gourmandise*, Cadiot-Badie on the Allées de Tourny and Saunion on the Cours Georges-Clemenceau rival each other for the quality of their chocolates. Coffee at the Brûlerie Gama behind the Porte-Dijeaux is roasted and blended on the spot.

Picnics can be a simple but tasty affair with local markets and shops providing all the necessary elements. Fillings for freshly baked *baguettes* – pork, chicken, duck and goose pâtés or *rillettes* – are often produced locally. Cured ham (*jambon de Bayonne*) is also much in evidence. Marmande tomatoes from neighbouring Lot-et-Garonne arrive in August and September, as do apples, pears and plums, all grown in the Entre-Deux-Mers.

Eating Out

Bordeaux has a good range of restaurants across the board, although the most choice is in the city itself. Country inns offer uncomplicated local dishes or *cuisine ménagère* at reasonable prices. Next step up are the restaurants producing regional fare and more elaborate dishes or *cuisine bourgeoise*. Finally, there is the more sophisticated cuisine of the Michelin-starred establishments, of which there are ten in the Bordeaux region. All have interesting fixed-price menus, particularly at lunch-time.

REGIONAL SPECIALITIES

Foie gras mi-cuit au sel Duck or goose liver cooked in a terrine and served cold in slices with warm toast and, traditionally, a glass of Sauternes.

Assiette de grenier médocain Cooked pork belly, rolled, sliced and served, normally, with a garnish of gelatine.

Huitres à la bordelaise Fresh oysters from the Bassin d'Arcachon, served with grilled flat, round sausages (known as *crépinettes*) and generously buttered bread.

Cèpes frais persillade Cèpe mushrooms sautéed with garlic and parsley. This can be served as a first course, but there are many recipes for cèpes as they are very popular in Bordeaux and are often used to garnish meat and game and in omelettes.

Alose grillée Shad that has been marinated in oil, onions and bay then grilled.

Lamproie à la bordelaise Lampreys marinated and cooked in red wine with onions, shallots, leeks, garlic, oil, bacon, herbs and Cognac. Ideally, the same wine used for the sauce should be drunk.

Rognons de veau à la bordelaise Lightly fried veal kidneys served in a *bordelaise* sauce made of red wine from Bordeaux, meat stock, marrow and shallots.

Agneau de Pauillac rôti aux gousses d'ail confites Roasted milk-fed lamb accompanied by cloves of garlic cooked in the meat juices.

Entrecôte à la bordelaise Sirloin steak traditionally grilled over *sarments*, or vine cuttings, and garnished with diced shallots.

Aiguillettes de canard aux navets Sautéed fine strips of duck breast served with turnips.

Bécasses au foie gras Roasted woodcock served on toast spread with puréed *foie gras*.

Pintade vigneronne Roasted guinea-fowl garnished with a bacon, shallots, bread and grape stuffing and served with grapes baked alongside the guinea-fowl.

Poulet bordelais Chicken pieces sautéed with parsley, shallots and crushed garlic.

Pruneaux au vin de Bordeaux Dried plums, or *Pruneaux d'Agen*, marinated for a couple of weeks in Sauternes and Armagnac.

Soupe de cerise au vin de Bordeaux Cherries poached in a sugar and water syrup then cooked in red wine. The *soupe* is then allowed to cool and is served slightly chilled.

Fanchonnets Almond *mille-feuille* and meringue pastries.

Cannelés girondins Small cone-shaped cakes flavoured with rum.

Touring Bordeaux

The Garonne is one of the two rivers in Bordeaux – the other is the Gironde – responsible for the mesoclimates that make Bordeaux's wines so special.

SUMMARY OF TOURS

Northern Médoc The first of a two-part trip through the Médoc, with visits to the grand châteaux in St-Julien, Pauillac and St-Estèphe, as well as to the more approachable estates in the north.

Southern Médoc Continues the voyage through the Médoc, discovering more great estates, including those of Margaux, as well as some of the lesser-known ACs.

Pessac-Léognan and Graves One of Bordeaux's oldest wine regions, with some vineyards now within the city's limits.

Sweet Wines of Bordeaux A visit to the most celebrated sweet wine region in the world, Sauternes.

Entre-Deux-Mers A less well-known region but one with a wealth of culture and value-for-money wines. Includes the Premières Côtes de Bordeaux.

St-Émilion The most famous name in Bordeaux and one of the most attractive regions, with its rolling landscape, medieval town and generous wines. Includes the St-Émilion satellites, and Côtes de Castillon and Bordeaux-Côtes de Francs.

Pomerol and Fronsac Discover voluptuous Pomerol, the underrated wines of Fronsac, with an optional excursion through the charming countryside of Bourg and Blaye.

The Romans established viticulture in this corner of south-west France, giving the Latin name Burdigala to a tiny settlement located on the Garonne river. Two thousand years on, Bordeaux, as it came to be known, is not only a great city in its own right, but is a name that is synonymous with wine.

Bordeaux produces more fine wine than any other area in the world, with over 110,000ha planted with vines. However, it is not just the magnitude of the region that is important, but its history, culture and, above all, the stature of its wines. The names Margaux, Graves, St-Émilion, Pomerol and Sauternes are famous around the world. The individual estates, Châteaux Haut-Brion, Latour and Margaux among others, represent the pinnacle of wine-making achievement. The tours provide a game-plan for a better understanding of this rich heritage.

Essential to touring in Bordeaux are good road maps and a certain amount of organization. The roads are all well maintained whether *autoroute*, *nationale* or *départementale*, but distances can be deceptive and signposting vague. The tours principally utilize country routes, but occasionally it may be necessary to cross the town of Libourne or circumnavigate Bordeaux city itself, perhaps using the busy ring road, the Rocade. The D2 'Route des Châteaux' winds past the major châteaux of the Médoc.

The vine comes to life in late April-early May and from then through to the end of the harvest in October is a good time to visit. Be warned, however, that most producers take their holidays in August and do not necessarily welcome visitors during the harvest months of September and October. The choice of accommodation in the wine country is limited, with the city of Bordeaux often providing a necessary base from which to make trips to the country. Bordeaux is one of France's gastronomic Meccas with a good range of restaurants.

There are a number of colourful festivals and other events throughout the Bordeaux region. These include the day-long *Fête du Printemps* in St-Émilion in June, when the oldest wine fraternity in Bordeaux, the Jurade de St-Émilion, gives its judgement on the latest vintage. The various ACs have also launched a series of Portes Ouvertes weekends, when château owners operate an open day for visitors to come to taste their wines. The international trade fair Vinexpo, which occurs every two years in June at Bordeaux-Lac, is a major event for the professional, providing an open stage for the wines of the world and a forum for commercial activity.

Bordeaux City

The Pont de Pierre was the first bridge to be built across the Garonne river in Bordeaux.

The city of Bordeaux is intrinsically linked to the region's wine industry. As far back as the Middle Ages the *Port de la Lune*, or Port of the Moon, situated on the curve of the Garonne river, was instrumental in establishing overseas trade routes. The city's rather grand 18th- and early 19th-century architecture is a reminder of its heyday, when the wine trade, along with other forms of commerce, brought great prosperity to Bordeaux. Today the port is of minor consequence, but the wines of Bordeaux are – now more than ever – an international commodity, with the city at the hub of this worldwide trade. Bordeaux is also the starting point for a pilgrimage into the surrounding wine regions and a shop window for their liquid wares.

The best place to start a walking tour of Bordeaux is at the Place de la Comédie, dominated by Victor Louis' impressive Grand Théâtre, one of the city's landmarks. Nearby, in the cours du XXX Juillet, is the Office du Tourisme and the Maison du Vin, both useful sources of information, and there are also a number of interesting wine shops in the vicinity, including la Vinotèque, Bordeaux Magnum and l'Intendant.

Walk along the vast Esplanade des Quinconces, and turn downstream (left) to the famous Quai des Chartrons, the trading quarter established in the 17th century by foreign wine merchants. Being located, at that time, outside the city walls, they avoided taxes on the export of wines. The city's merchants have long since abandoned the Quai for more cost-efficient premises, and today the only remaining link with the past is the Musée des Chartrons in the rue Borie, which houses an exhibition of wine paraphernalia.

Head back through the Esplanade to *le Triangle*, Bordeaux's exclusive shopping district, where there are several good food shops, including Dubernet for *foie gras*, Jean d'Alos for cheese and Cadiot-Badie and Saunion for chocolates. South of cours de l'Intendance, the rue Vital-Carles leads to the Cathédrale St-André, passing Mollat, a bookshop which has a large selection of wine, food and travel books in both English and French. This is the heart of the old city, one of the most fascinating areas to visit. Stroll down narrow lanes to Porte Cailhau, a turreted defensive gate built in the 15th century. Upstream is Bordeaux's first bridge, the Pont de Pierre – even more dramatic when lit at night. Return toward the Grand Théâtre via the Place du Parlement, with its choice of restaurants and the wine shop Cousin & Compagnie, open seven days a week. The Place de la Bourse facing the Garonne will be a final reminder of Bordeaux's 18th-century splendour.

Bordeaux City Fact File

The city of Bordeaux is the focal point for the region. There are hotels and restaurants to suit every pocket, providing an alternative to staying in the wine country.

Information

Librairie Mollat
15 rue Vital-Carles. Tel 05 56 40 40; fax 05 56 56 40 80.
Large general bookshop selling wine, food and travel guides in English as well as French.

Maison du Vin de Bordeaux
3 cours du XXX Juillet. Tel 05 56 00 22 88; fax 05 56 00 22 82.
Information for visiting the vineyards. Wine-tasting seminars also offered at the associated École du Vin du CIVB.

Musée des Chartrons
41 rue Borie. Tel 05 57 87 50 60; fax 05 56 79 10 98.
Permanent exhibition of wine-making materials.

Office du Tourisme
12 cours du XXX Juillet. Tel 05 56 00 66 00; fax 05 56 00 66 01.
Organizes visits to vineyards.

Markets
Marché des Capucins – daily
Marché des Grands Hommes – daily
Marché St-Michel – Saturday
Marché St-Pierre – Thursday

Festivals and Events
There are few wine festivals in the city of Bordeaux. One of the world's largest professional wine trade fairs, Vinexpo (tel 05 56 56 00 22), takes place at Bordeaux-Lac in June every other year. In May the *Foire Internationale de Bordeaux*, also held at Bordeaux-Lac, includes wine producers.

Where to Buy Wine
The selection is extensive but do not expect giveaway prices. Bargains can be had at the *Foires des Vins*, organized by the large supermarkets at the end of September.

Baud et Millet
19 rue Huguerie.
Cheese specialist with wine shop.

Bordeaux's elegant shops provide a showcase for the region's wines – but search around for the best value.

Bordeaux Magnum
3 rue Gobineau.
Bottles as well as magnums are available.

Cousin & Compagnie
Place du Parlement.
Open 7 days a week from 11am–10pm.

L'Intendant
2 allées de Tourny.
Over 700 châteaux to choose from, ranged around a spiral stairway. Stock includes some older vintages.

La Vinothèque de Bordeaux
8 cours du XXX Juillet.
More than 200 châteaux represented.

Where to Stay and Eat

Hôtel Burdigala Ⓗ
115 rue Georges-Bonnac. Tel 05 56 90 16 16; fax 05 56 93 15 06. ⒻⒻⒻ
Modern, international hotel, with spacious rooms and excellent service.

Restaurant le Chapon Fin Ⓡ
5 rue Montesquieu. Tel 05 56 79 10 10; fax 05 56 79 09 10. ⒻⒻⒻ
Refined cuisine and extensive wine list with older vintages.

Hôtel Etche Ona Ⓗ
11 rue Mautrec. Tel 05 56 44 36 49; fax 05 56 44 59 58. Ⓕ
Simple establishment centrally located near the Place de la Comédie.

Restaurant Jean Ramet Ⓡ
7–8 place Jean Jaurès. Tel 05 56 44 12 51. ⒻⒻⒻ
Small, intimate restaurant favoured by the locals. Fish, game and desserts are specialities.

Hôtel de Normandie Ⓗ
7–9 cours du XXX Juillet. Tel 05 56 52 16 80; fax 05 56 51 68 91. ⒻⒻ
Located in an 18th-century building next to the Maison du Vin.

Restaurant la Petite Brasserie Ⓡ
43 rue du Pas St-Georges. Tel 05 56 52 19 79. Ⓕ
Simple regional fare and Bordeaux's Grands Crus offered at attractive prices.

Hôtel de Sèze Ⓗ
7 rue de Sèze. Tel 05 56 52 65 54; fax 05 56 44 31 83. ⒻⒻ
Charming, comfortable hotel with 24 rooms in an elegant quarter of Bordeaux.

Bistro du Sommelier Ⓡ
163 rue Georges-Bonnac. Tel 05 56 96 71 78; fax 05 56 24 52 36. Ⓕ
Fast-moving wine list offered at retail prices.

Restaurant la Tupina Ⓡ
6 rue Porte de la Monnaie. Tel 05 56 91 56 37; fax 05 56 31 92 11. ⒻⒻ
Bistro with homely décor serving regional cuisine. *Foie gras*, duck and game specialities, with a comprehensive wine list.

Restaurant le Vieux Bordeaux Ⓡ
27 rue Buhan. Tel 05 56 52 94 36; fax 05 56 44 25 11. ⒻⒻ
Located in the old part of the city. Refined regional cuisine with a slight Spanish influence and well-chosen wine list.

Northern Médoc

Since the mid-1980s the wines of Troisième Cru Ch. Lagrange have benefited from massive investment.

There is probably no other region in the world that has such a concentration of high-profile estates as this part of the Médoc. Pauillac boasts three Premiers Crus, Châteaux Lafite-Rothschild, Latour and Mouton-Rothschild, as well as other prominent châteaux. The Crus Classés of St-Julien represent three-quarters of the AC, maintaining a uniformly high level of quality, and St-Estèphe, although not revelling in 'stars', has an excellent group of properties.

Around St-Yzans-de-Médoc the terrain in the Bas-Médoc (better known as Médoc AC) becomes scenically more pleasing but is less able to produce truly great wines. The châteaux, however, are freely accessible to visitors and the wines often attractive and affordable. As in the higher profile communal ACs, mainly red wines are produced.

The Tour

St-Laurent-Médoc is the starting point of the tour and can be reached from Bordeaux via the N215. From here, turn due east toward St-Julien-Beychevelle. This is the initial vineyard area of Haut-Médoc AC, and rows of vines and patches of woodland extend on both sides of the road. After the moated medieval château of la Tour-Carnet and Ch. Belgrave, a wide, open expanse of gravelly vineyard announces the western limits of St-Julien AC. This communal AC is divided from Haut-Médoc AC by an almost indiscernible stream, the Riou Cla, which, along with the Jalle du Nord further south, provides effective drainage.

Ch. Lagrange is the first estate on this open plateau, its 18th-century château nestling in a copse. Unusually in the Médoc, the vineyard lies in one single block of 113ha, and benefits from natural and man-made drainage systems. The cellars are spick and span, and since the 1983 takeover by the Japanese drinks group Suntory, the wines have been one of the revelations of the AC.

The road continues eastward through gently undulating vineyards past Deuxième Cru Ch. Gruaud-Larose, which produces one of the most powerful wines in St-Julien. On entering the village of Beychevelle a larger-than-life bottle labelled 'Grand Vin de St-Julien-Médoc' stands at a cross-roads, with Ch. St-Pierre, source of good-value wines, to one side. In the distance, beyond the square towers of Ch. Ducru-Beaucaillou, which produces truly elegant wines of great distinction, is the ever-present Gironde estuary. The road south leads to the striking 18th-century estate of Ch. Beychevelle, with its seductive, supple style of wine, but turning north past the unclassified but notable Ch. Gloria, it dips and turns into a slight hollow, arriving at the gates of

TOUR SUMMARY

Starting in St-Laurent-Médoc, the tour heads via St-Julien, Pauillac and St-Estèphe to some of the hard-working estates of Médoc AC in the north, and finishes in Lesparre-Médoc.

Distance covered 80km (50 miles).

Time needed 6 hours.

Terrain The route is almost entirely confined to narrow, easy-to-drive *départementale* roads.

Hotels Apart from a couple of top-quality hotels, the choice is limited. Look to the city of Bordeaux and southern Médoc for other options.

Restaurants There are two top restaurants, but few good regional establishments. Picnicking is a good option in the summer.

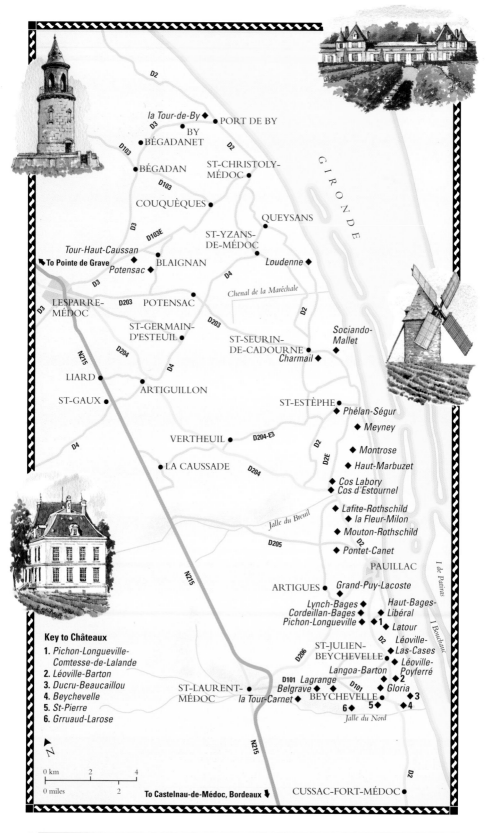

D2

la Tour-de-By ◆ ● PORT DE BY
D3
BY
● BÉGADANET
D103 **D2**

BÉGADAN ● ST-CHRISTOLY-
MÉDOC ●
D103

COUQUÈQUES ● ●

QUEYSANS
D3
D103E ST-YZANS-
DE-MÉDOC
Tour-Haut-Caussan ◆ ●
➤ To Pointe de Grave ● ● BLAIGNAN ● Loudenne ◆
Potensac ◆
D3 **D4**

LESPARRE- **D203** POTENSAC Chenal de la Maréchale
MÉDOC
D3 **D2**
D203
ST-GERMAIN-
D'ESTEUIL ●
D204 ST-SEURIN-
DE-CADOURNE Sociando-
Charmail ◆ Mallet
◆
N215 **D4**
LIARD ●
ARTIGUILLON
ST-GAUX ●
ST-ESTÈPHE ●
◆ Phélan-Ségur

◆ Meyney
VERTHEUIL ● **D204-E3**
D2 ◆ Montrose
D4 **D2E**
● LA CAUSSADE **D204** ◆ Haut-Marbuzet

◆ Cos Labory
◆ Cos d'Estournel

◆ Lafite-Rothschild
◆ la Fleur-Milon
Jalle du Breuil
◆ Mouton-Rothschild
D205
◆ Pontet-Canet

PAUILLAC

N215 ARTIGUES ● Grand-Puy-Lacoste ◆

Lynch-Bages ◆ Haut-Bages-
Cordeillan-Bages ◆ Libéral
Pichon-Longueville ◆ ◆ 1 ◆ Latour

Léoville-
D2 ◆ Las-Cases
Key to Châteaux ST-JULIEN-
1. Pichon-Longueville- BEYCHEVELLE ◆ ◆ Léoville-
   Comtesse-de-Lalande **D206** Langoa-Barton Poyferré
2. Léoville-Barton Lagrange ◆ ◆ 2
3. Ducru-Beaucaillou **D101** **D101** ◆ Gloria
4. Beychevelle ST-LAURENT- Belgrave ◆ ◆
5. St-Pierre MÉDOC la Tour-Carnet ◆ BEYCHEVELLE ◆ 3
6. Grruaud-Larose 6 ◆ 5 ◆ 4
Jalle du Nord

N

0 km 2   4
0 miles   2

To Castelnau-de-Médoc, Bordeaux ⬇ CUSSAC-FORT-MÉDOC ●

D2

GIRONDE

Chenal de la Maréchale

l de Patiras

l Bouchaut

Ch. Langoa-Barton. This Troisième Cru shares wine-making facilities with Deuxième Cru Ch. Léoville-Barton – both are owned and managed by Anthony Barton and his daughter Lilian, from one of Bordeaux's oldest wine trade families. The wines are vinified in large oak vats, the character of each dictated by the vineyards from which they originated. Those of Léoville-Barton have a more southerly exposure and are further from the water table, which helps to give a little more firmness and structure to the wines, making them extremely long-lived. Langoa-Barton, with north-facing vineyards, is a softer wine, the St-Julien fruit character expressed earlier.

Catch a glimpse of Ch. Langoa-Barton's beautiful rose garden before heading north again past the Léoville vineyards, which in the 18th century formed the largest single estate in the Médoc. The stone cellars of Châteaux Léoville-Las-Cases and Léoville-Poyferré monopolize the village of St-Julien. Both are excellent wines, with Las-Cases unofficially ranked alongside the Premiers Crus. Leaving the village, a wrought-iron gateway gives a sneak preview of the continuation of the Las-Cases vineyards and then, around a bend, the stone arch with lion, depicted on the wine labels, leaps into view.

An archway topped by a stone lion guards the vineyards of Deuxième Cru Ch. Léoville-Las-Cases.

Pause here to admire the magnificent panorama. A stone wall outlines the vineyards of Ch. Léoville-Las-Cases. Just beyond, a small stream marks the boundary between the St-Julien and Pauillac ACs, with the solitary 18th-century domed tower of Ch. Latour close by. On the brow of a small hill Châteaux Pichon-Longueville and Pichon-Longueville-Comtesse-de-Lalande stand facing each other. To the east the Gironde becomes more of a presence, proving the saying in the Médoc that all the best vineyards can 'see' the estuary. To the west a carpet of vines unrolls along a plateau heading toward stately Ch. Grand-Puy-Lacoste.

As you turn into the drive that leads to Ch. Latour, Pauillac's deep gravel soils are immediately apparent. The other factors that make Latour such a powerful wine are perhaps less obvious: a rich clay bedrock helps produce the intensity; ridges of vineyard that slope gently to the east catch the sun's early morning rays; and the proximity of the Gironde provides a warm mesoclimate that protects against frost and allows Cabernet Sauvignon to ripen successfully. There is no grandiose château here, but each vintage provides a monument to this classic estate.

Heading north again, the road passes between the two Pichons, then continues past the much-improved Ch. Haut-Bages-Libéral. On the outskirts of Pauillac, near the vineyards of Ch. Lynch-Bages, the luxury hotel and restaurant Ch. Cordeillan-Bages provides a comfortable setting for a stop. Alternatively, take the road down to Pauillac's

Map illustrations: (above left) Ch. la Tour-de-By; (above right) Ch. Loudenne; (centre) the windmill at Caussan; (below) Ch. Latour.

quayside past the Maison du Vin, and settle for a simple meal at one of the cafés overlooking the harbour.

Continue along the waterfront, crossing a railway line to climb again into gravelly vineyard. This is the second of Pauillac's two viticultural plateaux, home to the notable châteaux of Lafite-Rothschild, Mouton-Rothschild, Pontet-Canet and the more obscure but good-value la Fleur-Milon. At a wayside cross the road branches off toward Ch. Mouton-Rothschild. There is no striking château but a wooded park, stark white *chai* and a museum containing ancient wine artefacts from around the world. The wines, almost pure Cabernet Sauvignon, are dark, rich and exotic.

The vineyards of Ch. Mouton-Rothschild adjoin those of Ch. Lafite-Rothschild, but access to this estate is via the hamlet of le Pouyalet. Running downhill, the road passes the steeply sloping vineyards of Lafite to arrive at the château and its rambling cellar complex. The Rothschilds' personal inventory of old vintages dates back to 1797. A more recent addition has been the unconventional circular barrel cellar built in 1987. The wines of Ch. Lafite have a distinct personality – elegant, firm and long-lived.

The estate stands close to the southern limits of St-Estèphe and, unusually, has a parcel of vines in this AC. Crossing over the Jalle du Breuil and through a small stretch of meadow, the road climbs to the lieu-dit of Cos, which in ancient Gascon means 'Hill of Pebbles'. A solitary tower stands on one side of the road, and on the other, as the road rises around the bend, the extraordinary 'pagoda' form of Ch. Cos d'Estournel. As well as viewing the château's remarkable architecture and tasting the rich, concentrated wines produced on these well-drained soils, it is worth visiting the small museum. Right next door is Ch. Cos Labory, whose wines are very good and reasonably priced.

Turning toward the Gironde the slopes become more accentuated, the vineyards rising and falling at diverse angles and the soils a mix of limestone, clay, gravel and sand – hence the variety of styles of wine. The road meanders northwards, passing one of the star Crus Bourgeois of the AC, Ch. Haut-Marbuzet. Like neighbouring Ch. Montrose, the ivy-clad Ch. Meyney overlooks the estuary. It has gravelly soils on a limestone bedrock and produces a typically concentrated, slightly austere style of St-Estèphe. Within the village of St-Estèphe itself is the imposing estate of Phélan-Ségur, now making excellent wines.

Take the road that runs alongside the estuary past tiny fishermen's huts, twisting and turning its way through flat meadows to St-Seurin-de-Cadourne. Just before the village the road rises to the vineyards of Ch. Sociando-Mallet; this is located on an outcrop of gravelly soils identical to those of

The Star of David marks the cellars of Ch. Mouton-Rothschild, an estate with a reputation for flamboyant wine labels as well as for its rich and powerful wines.

the best vineyards of the communal ACs and consequently makes superb wines under Haut-Médoc AC. Neighbouring Ch. Charmail is a new star, and is excellent value.

Fishermen's huts on stilts and cantilevered nets are a common sight in the northern Médoc. The Gironde river creates a warm mesoclimate, which benefits the vineyards close to it.

North of St-Seurin, the Haut-Médoc vineyards are interspersed with farmland. Over to the west the meadows and marshland are a reminder that, until the Dutch drained the Médoc in the 17th century, this was a rather wretched, waterlogged part of the world. As the road descends and crosses the Chenal de la Maréchale, so Médoc AC begins. On an isolated hillock overlooking the Gironde stands the pink chartreuse of Ch. Loudenne. The mixed gravel and clay soils on this ridge produce both red and white wines. Ch. Loudenne is also a veritable wine centre, with visits to the museum, wine school and cellars encouraged.

Toward St-Christoly-Médoc the countryside becomes increasingly rural. North and south of the village gravel soils return and the vineyards reappear. The most impressive property here, with a reputation for consistency dating back to the 18th century, is Ch. la Tour-de-By. Today the Pagès family maintain this excellent tradition, while an ancient stone lighthouse announces the proximity of the Gironde.

Inland, toward Lesparre-Médoc, vineyards once more alternate with farmland and forest. Several properties around Bégadan and Blaignan produce attractive wines from vines grown on clay, limestone and gravel soils. The Courrian family has lived in Blaignan since 1634, and today at Ch. Tour-Haut-Caussan, Philippe Courrian produces an excellent Cabernet Sauvignon-Merlot blend. The windmill that appears on the label is a working reality and can be seen at Caussan. Immediately south of Blaignan is Ch. Potensac, probably the best-value wine in Médoc AC. To finish the tour, head to Lesparre-Médoc and pick up the N215 back to Bordeaux, or spend a night in the peaceful Médoc.

Northern Médoc Fact File

Apart from two excellent hotel/restaurants, the choice in the northern Médoc is limited. The *Guide Découverte* for the Médoc, available from the Maisons du Vin and renewed yearly, offers useful information on the châteaux and the region. For further information refer to the Southern Médoc Fact File (p.28) and Bordeaux City Fact File (p.14).

Information

École du Vin
Château Loudenne, 33340 St-Yzans-de-Médoc. Tel 05 56 09 05 03; fax 05 56 09 02 87. Residential wine courses run in English and French.

Maison du Tourisme et du Vin de Médoc
La Verrerie, 33250 Pauillac. Tel 05 56 59 03 08; fax 05 56 59 23 38. Information, tastings and wine tours; also stocks wines available for purchase.

Maison du Vin de St-Estèphe
Place de l'Église, 33180 St-Estèphe. Tel 05 56 59 30 59; fax 05 56 59 73 72. Wines available for purchase.

Syndicat Viticole des Appellations Médoc et Haut-Médoc
18 quai Jean Fleuret, 33250 Pauillac. Tel 05 56 59 30 59.

Markets
Pauillac – Saturday
Lesparre-Médoc – Tuesday and Saturday

Festivals and Events
A Portes Ouvertes weekend is organized in April throughout the Médoc. The *Marathon du Médoc*, in September, is a major event with a route that passes over 50 prestigious châteaux. Three notable festivals are organized by the Commanderie du Bontemps de Médoc et des Graves: *Fête de St-Vincent*, the patron saint of vinegrowers, in January; *Fête de la Fleur* in June to celebrate the flowering of the vines; and the *Ban des Vendanges* in September, to mark the official start of the harvest. These are by invitation only.

Wrapping by hand adds the finishing touch to this bottle of 1949 Premier Cru Ch. Latour.

Where to Buy Wine
Wines can generally be bought direct from the châteaux throughout Médoc AC, but the best buys are to be found in the supermarkets. The Cru Classé châteaux sometimes have a limited selection available by the bottle.

Cave la Pauillacaise
Le Pouyalet, 33250 Pauillac. Stocks château-bottled wines as well as an interesting selection by the litre (*en vrac*) of communal AC wines.

Where to Stay and Eat

Hôtel/Restaurant Château Cordeillan-Bages ⒽⓇ
33250 Pauillac. Tel 05 56 59 24 24; fax 05 56 59 01 89. ⒻⒻⒻ Situated on the outskirts of Pauillac, this is the best hotel in the Médoc. There are spacious rooms, while the restaurant serves refined cuisine and has a comprehensive wine list. The hotel also runs an École du Bordeaux, which offers wine appreciation classes.

Hôtel/Restaurant Château Layauga ⒽⓇ
33340 Gaillan-Médoc. Tel 05 56 41 26 83; fax 05 56 41 19 52. ⒻⒻⒻ Star-rated establishment with 7 comfortable rooms and inspired regional cuisine. Good wine list.

Hôtel Château Pomys Ⓗ
33180 St-Estèphe. Tel 05 56 59 73 44. ⒻⒻ Attractive 19th-century château offering bed and breakfast accommodation.

Hôtel de France et d'Angleterre ⒽⓇ
3 quai Albert-Pichon. 33250 Pauillac. Tel 05 56 59 01 20; fax 05 56 59 02 31. ⒻⒻ On the quayside in Pauillac. Snug rooms and restaurant with fixed-price menus. Adequate wine list.

Bar/Restaurant le Peyrat Ⓡ
Port de la Chapelle, 33180 St-Estèphe. Tel 05 56 59 71 43. Ⓕ Modest bar by the estuary serving simple dishes.

Hôtel/Restaurant la Renaissance ⒽⓇ
33120 St-Laurent-Médoc. Tel 05 56 59 40 29. Ⓕ Village restaurant serving regional cuisine. Ten rooms.

Restaurant le St-Julien Ⓡ
2 rue des Acacias – Place St-Julien, 33250 St-Julien-Beychevelle. Tel 05 56 59 63 87; fax 05 56 59 63 89. ⒻⒻ Opened in 1996 in a renovated stone building. Classic cuisine and serious wine list.

Hôtel des Vieux Acacias Ⓗ
33340 Queyrac. Tel 05 56 59 80 63; fax 05 56 59 85 93. ⒻⒻ To the north of the peninsula, 20 comfortable rooms offered in a peaceful setting.

Auberge des Vignobles Ⓡ
33340 Blaignan. Tel 05 56 09 04 81. Ⓕ Simple country inn located in the hamlet of Caussan.

Wines and Wine Villages

There is only one reason to tour the northern Médoc and that is to admire the grand châteaux. Scenically the region has less to offer, although the countryside in the north of the peninsula has a little more charm.

Crus Classés The 1855 Classification for red wines consists entirely of Médoc properties (with the exception of Haut-Brion). There are 5 Crus and the order denotes the rank within each level:

Premiers Crus: Latour, Lafite-Rothschild, Margaux, Haut-Brion, Mouton-Rothschild (since 1973).

Deuxièmes Crus: Rauzan-Ségla, Rauzan-Gassies, Léoville-Las-Cases, Léoville-Poyferré, Léoville-Barton, Durfort-Vivens, Lascombes, Gruaud-Larose, Brane-Cantenac, Pichon-Longueville, Pichon-Longueville-Comtesse-de-Lalande, Ducru-Beaucaillou, Cos d'Estournel, Montrose.

Troisièmes Crus: Giscours, Kirwan, d'Issan, Lagrange, Langoa-Barton, Malescot-St-Exupéry, Cantenac-Brown, Palmer, la Lagune, Desmirail, Calon-Ségur, Ferrière, Marquis d'Alesme-Becker, Boyd-Cantenac.

Quatrièmes Crus: St-Pierre, Branaire, Talbot, Duhart-Milon, Pouget, la Tour-Carnet, Lafon-Rochet, Beychevelle, Prieuré-Lichine, Marquis-de-Terme.

Cinquièmes Crus: Pontet-Canet, Batailley, Grand-Puy-Lacoste, Grand-Puy-Ducasse, Haut-Batailley, Lynch-Bages, Lynch-Moussas, Dauzac, d'Armailhac (formerly Mouton-Baronne-Philippe), du Tertre, Haut-Bages-Libéral, Pédesclaux, Belgrave, Camensac, Cos Labory, Clerc-Milon, Croizet-Bages, Cantemerle.

Haut-Médoc AC See p.29.

Médoc AC Red wines only, covering the northern part of the Médoc peninsula, with vineyards from St-Yzans-de-Médoc through to Jau-Dignac-et-Loirac. Soils vary from lighter gravel outcrops to limestone and clay. The wines have a full fruit character, often with a dominance of Merlot in the classic Bordeaux blend. New oak barrels are used at some estates. *Best producers:* Greysac, Lacombe-Noaillac, LOUDENNE, Noaillac, les Ormes-Sorbet, Patache d'Aux, Plagnac, Potensac, Rollan-de-By, LA TOUR-DE-BY, TOUR-HAUT-CAUSSAN, la Tour-St-Bonnet, Vieux-Robin.

Pauillac AC Communal AC centred around Pauillac, undeclared viticultural 'capital' of the Médoc. The co-operative, la Rose Pauillac, is in the town.

The AC has 3 Premiers Crus and 15 other Crus Classés (see above). Cabernet Sauvignon, grown on deep gravel soils, provides the basis for these firmly structured, sappy, long-lived wines, and for the characteristic blackcurrant, cedarwood and mineral bouquet. *Best producers:* Batailley, la Bécasse, Clerc-Milon, Duhart-Milon, Fonbadet, Grand-Puy-Lacoste, Haut-Bages-Libéral, Haut-Batailley, LAFITE-ROTHSCHILD, LATOUR, LYNCH-BAGES, MOUTON-ROTHSCHILD, Pibran, PICHON-LONGUEVILLE, PICHON-LONGUEVILLE-COMTESSE-DE-LALANDE, *Pontet-Canet.*

St-Estèphe AC The most northerly of the communal ACs and, as the largest, the rival to Margaux. Soils vary considerably, with zones of gravel, limestone, clay and sand – hence the less uniform style. Cabernet is the principal grape, although Merlot figures heavily in a number of wines. The classic St-Estèphe is robust, sometimes austere with plenty of fruit concentration. There are 5 Cru Classés. *Best producers:* Calon-Ségur, COS D'ESTOURNEL, Cos Labory, le Crock, Haut-Marbuzet, Lafon-Rochet, Lilian-Ladouys, MEYNEY, MONTROSE, les Ormes-de-Pez, de Pez, Phélan-Ségur.

St-Julien AC The smallest of the 4 communal ACs, with about 900ha of vines. Three-quarters of the vineyard area is held by Crus Classés, which uniformly produce top-quality wines. The gravel and clay soils impart a rich texture and have attractive fruit, with the heavier soils to the west producing a fuller style, those closer to the estuary more finesse. *Best producers:* BEYCHEVELLE, Branaire, Ducru-Beaucaillou, Gloria, Gruaud-Larose, LAGRANGE, LANGOA-BARTON, LÉOVILLE-BARTON, LÉOVILLE-LAS-CASES, Léoville-Poyferré, St-Pierre, Talbot, Terrey-Gros-Cailloux.

A stunning display of flowers spells out the name of Ch. Beychevelle, a Quatrième Cru in St-Julien AC.

The vaulted *chai*, or cellar, at Ch. Margaux is where wines spend their second year of maturation. The temperature is kept at 15°C (59°F) and humidity is maintained at 85 per cent. The upright barriques are new and empty, awaiting transfer to the first year cellar above for reception of the new vintage. Margaux is aged in 100 per cent new oak barrels and the second wine, Pavillon Rouge, in 50 per cent, resulting in an intake each year of approximately 1500 new oak barriques of 225 litres – the classic Bordeaux size. The small cooperage at Ch. Margaux produces 30 per cent of the estate's requirements.

Southern Médoc

Merlot grapes – here, being harvested at Ch. Lamarque in the Haut-Médoc, are an important element of the Bordeaux blend.

Map illustrations: (above) the church at Moulis-en-Médoc; (centre) Ch. Lamarque; (below) Ch. d'Issan.

TOUR SUMMARY

Heading north from Bordeaux, this tour explores the famous châteaux of Margaux. The route also takes in the lesser-known but quality-orientated châteaux of Moulis and Listrac; there is an optional detour to Arsac.

Distance covered 100km (60 miles) not including detour.

Time needed 6 hours; allow an extra hour for detour.

Terrain The tour mainly uses the D2 'Route des Châteaux', which runs parallel to the Gironde estuary. It can be slow moving but easy to drive.

Hotels There is a limited choice of accommodation within the southern Médoc. The city of Bordeaux and northern Médoc offer additional options.

Restaurants Local restaurants of varying price categories offer an adequate choice.

Margaux forms the core of the southern Médoc and is the nearest of the great communal ACs to the city of Bordeaux. It is a name that evokes a variety of sentiments. For many, the wines of Margaux are the epitome of subtlety and elegance, as portrayed by those of Ch. Margaux. For others, it has been a disappointment in recent years, the quality of the wines falling short of their noble reputation. The region is extensive and the potential to produce great wines is still there. The tour visits a number of the 21 Cru Classé estates to see the efforts being made to maintain or regain the AC's prestige.

North and south of Margaux, estates produce wines in Haut-Médoc AC; further inland at Moulis and Listrac are two more quality ACs, where the vine has been cultivated since the Middle Ages, but neither received any accolades in the 1855 Classification and both remain obscure compared to their communal cousins. The geographical conditions are varied, but the wines distinctive – at times even great.

The Tour

Head north out of Bordeaux into the Médoc. Leave the Rocade at Exit 7 in the direction of le Verdon, then turn off on to the D2 'Route des Châteaux'. Bordeaux's suburban sprawl first gives way to pine forest and flat scrub land, typical of most of the Médoc. Finally, the road breaks out into the vineyards of Ch. la Lagune, the first Cru Classé after Bordeaux. There is a slight undulation in the terrain here, and the soils have a percentage of the famous Médoc gravel, so important for good drainage and for retaining heat. The mix of fine gravel and sand found in this part of the Haut-Médoc also helps to produce wines of surprising finesse.

A little further north lies the other important Cru Classé of the southern Médoc, Ch. Cantemerle, producer since the early 1980s of ripe, supple, aromatic wines. However, a detour via Ludon-Médoc allows a glimpse of a cooperage, the Tonnelerie Ludonnaise. Stacks of barrel staves lie weathering in the open air over 2ha of land, and inside the cooperage more than 20,000 barriques bordelais a year are made for use around the world.

North of Macau the road draws closer to the Gironde estuary. A detour to Arsac in the west, one of the five communes that make up Margaux AC, offers the option of visiting the outstanding but unclassified estates of Ch. Monbrison, and Ch. du Tertre, located on a gravel rise and the only Cru Classé in the commune, before returning to the D2 via Ch. d'Angludet, an excellent Cru Bourgeois and the property of English négociant Peter Sichel.

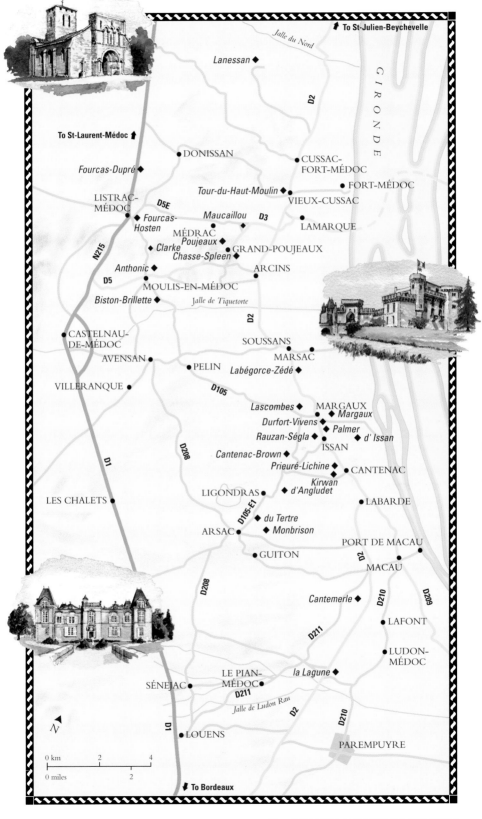

The main tour continues north, rejoining the D2, and enters Margaux AC at the commune of Labarde. The vineyards at last begin to creep into view, hemmed in on the west by pine forest and on the east by marshy meadow. After dipping underneath the railway line at Cantenac, a tiny track leads to Ch. Kirwan, named after an Irish merchant who owned the property in the latter part of the 18th century. Looking north-west toward the Queen Anne-styled folly of Ch. Cantenac-Brown, the undulating gravel hillocks of Cantenac come into full view. Ch. Kirwan has vineyards on this well-sited terrain and is now beginning to make the most of them, having applied greater precision and selectivity to its wine-making process.

The D2 continues past the ancient ivy-covered priory of Ch. Prieuré-Lichine and disappears into the rolling epicentre of the Margaux vineyards. The ground is strewn with pebbles and appears bright with the quantity of fine Garonne gravel, ideal soil for producing great wines. Approaching the village of Issan, the conical turrets of Ch. Palmer, with the British, Dutch and French flags of its joint ownership, appear, officially a Troisième Cru, but consistently produces wines of higher distinction. The eponymous Ch. d'Issan is further to the east.

The wines of elegant Ch. Margaux represent the height of achievement for Margaux AC.

Beyond is the village of Margaux and, near the church, the imposing 19th-century colonnaded building of Ch. Margaux. A great percentage of its vineyards are on deep gravel soils, perfect for ripening Cabernet Sauvignon: the wines are consequently rich and dense but have all the elegance and finesse expected from a great Margaux. After an indifferent spell in the 1960s and 70s, the estate's fortunes were revived following a change of ownership in 1978. New ownership has also added momentum to the revival at nearby Ch. Rauzan-Ségla, where one of the improving projects has been the laying of 14km (9 miles) of drainage pipes.

The tiny village of Margaux is packed with the grandiose 18th- and 19th-century châteaux of a host of Cru Classé estates. In the hands of the youthful Gonzague Lurton, Ch. Durfort-Vivens is beginning to make much-improved wines and Ch. Lascombes, owned by Bass Charrington, is welcoming to visitors. After stopping for lunch, perhaps at le Savoie, head north again, plunging back into vineyards. The road winds past Ch. Labégorce-Zédé, another excellent non-classified property, located on the edge of Soussans, the most northerly Margaux commune.

After Soussans the vineyards peter out and the landscape returns to pine forest and meadow. There are, however, outcrops of gravelly soil that provide excellent vineyard land and good-value châteaux, which produce wine under the Haut-Médoc AC. In Vieux-Cussac, Ch. Tour-du-Haut-Moulin makes wines of depth and consistency. Further north

Ch. Lanessan has long been considered a fine estate. It stands in rambling parkland with the vineyards overlooking those of Ch. Beychevelle in neighbouring St-Julien.

Retracing the route back to Lamarque, turn west toward Moulis and Listrac. On entering Moulis AC, the landscape again becomes one of vines planted on gently undulating gravel soils. Near the village of Grand-Poujeaux the gravelly Garonne soils are identical to those found in Margaux and St-Julien, and so it is no surprise to find that the leading châteaux in the AC, Chasse-Spleen, Maucaillou and Poujeaux, are located here.

South-west of Grand-Poujeaux the road dips away into trees and meadow and reappears in vineyards close to the village of Moulis-en-Médoc. Here the soils are clay-limestone and the warming influence of the Gironde is less apparent. The grapes ripen later and it is more difficult to make classic wines, although dynamic châteaux like Anthonic and Biston-Brillette have proved that good wine-making practices can produce excellent results in this terrain.

Passing the village's 12th-century church, turn toward Listrac-Médoc. The road winds past Ch. Clarke, a completely renovated property owned by Baron Edmond de Rothschild. The Grand-Listrac co-operative stands squarely in the village. To the north the lieu-dit le Fourcas is just about the highest point in the Médoc – although at 43m (140ft) this is almost imperceptible. There is an outcrop of Pyrenean gravel here and Château Fourcas-Hosten and Fourcas-Dupré make typically firm Listrac wines from a high percentage of Cabernet Sauvignon. The busy N215 also runs through the village, providing a swift passage back to Bordeaux or north to St-Julien and Pauillac.

Ch. Rauzan-Ségla has been revamped from head to toe since its 1994 purchase by Chanel.

Southern Médoc Fact File

Despite the number of tourists, southern Médoc remains a quiet, rural area. The choice of hotels and restaurants has grown, but is still not extensive. See also Northern Médoc Fact File (p.20) and Bordeaux City Fact File (p.14).

Information

Maison du Vin de Margaux
Place la Trémoille, 33460 Margaux. Tel 05 57 88 70 82. The *Guide Découverte* for the Médoc is a useful booklet, and there is also a small selection of wines available.

Musée des Arts et Métiers de la Vigne et du Vin
Espace Maucaillou, 33480 Moulis-en-Médoc. Tel 05 56 58 01 23; fax 05 56 58 00 88.

Syndicat Viticole de Listrac
Ch. Saransot-Dupré, 33480 Listrac-Médoc. Tel 05 56 58 03 02; fax 05 56 58 07 64.

Syndicat Viticole de Moulis
Ch. Maucaillou, 33480 Moulis-en-Médoc. Tel 05 56 58 05 16; fax 05 56 58 00 88.

Tonnelerie Ludonnaise
12 rue Lafon, 33290 Ludon-Médoc. Tel 05 57 88 16 06; fax 05 57 88 48 95. Interesting cooperage where barriques bordelais are made. Visits by appointment only.

Markets

Lamarque – first Thursday in the month
Ludon-Médoc – Saturday

Festivals and Events

See Northern Médoc Fact File (p.20).

Where to Buy Wine

Wines can seldom be bought at the Cru Classé châteaux, although some may have one or two vintages for sale by the bottle. Prices are no better than from a regular wine shop. Châteaux in the Haut-Médoc, Listrac and Moulis ACs are generally happier about cellar door sales and sometimes offer older vintages no longer available on the open market.

Although not a Cru Classé, Ch. Chasse-Spleen is nevertheless one of the best properties of Moulis AC.

Where to Stay and Eat

Château Cap-Léon-Veyrin Ⓗ
33480 Listrac-Médoc. Tel 05 56 58 07 28; fax 05 56 58 07 50. Ⓕ
Bed and breakfast available at this creditable wine-producing estate.

Chez Quinquin Ⓡ
33460 Port de Macau. Tel 05 57 88 45 89. Ⓕ
Mussels, oysters and other seafood dishes can be sampled at this open-air café on the bank of the Garonne river.

Domaine des Sapins Ⓗ
Lieu-dit Bouqueyran, 33480 Moulis-en-Médoc. Tel 05 56 58 18 26. Ⓕ
Bed and breakfast in this small country retreat. Six rooms available and dinner if booked in advance.

Restaurant Larigaudière Ⓡ
Soussans, 33460 Margaux. Tel 05 57 88 74 02; fax 05 57 88 33 72. Ⓕ
Regional fare with a selection of set price menus served in an agreeable setting.

Restaurant le Lion d'Or Ⓡ
33460 Arcins-en-Médoc. Tel 05 56 58 96 79. Ⓕ Ⓕ
Country-style cooking done

with real flair. Agneau de Pauillac is a regular dish, otherwise the menu has a seasonal flavour. Unusually for France, you can bring your own bottle of wine.

Relais de Margaux Ⓗ Ⓡ
33460 Margaux. Tel 05 57 88 38 30; fax 05 57 88 31 73. Ⓕ Ⓕ Ⓕ
Luxury hotel offering a range of modern conveniences. Competent cuisine and comprehensive wine list.

Relais du Médoc Ⓡ
33460 Lamarque. Tel 05 56 58 92 27. Ⓕ
Village inn offering regional fare.

Auberge Médocaine
33480 Listrac-Médoc. Tel 05 56 58 08 86. Ⓕ
Simple country food and an inexpensive lunchtime buffet menu.

Restaurant l'Orée du Médoc Ⓗ Ⓡ
33480 Listrac-Médoc. Tel 05 56 58 08 68; fax 05 56 58 08 68. Ⓕ
Small bistro offering regional dishes. Some rooms available on a bed and breakfast basis.

Hôtel/Restaurant le Pavillon de Margaux Ⓗ Ⓡ
33460 Margaux. Tel 05 57 88 77 54; fax 05 57 88 77 73. Ⓕ Ⓕ
Opened in 1996 with 10 comfortable rooms. Classic cuisine served overlooking the vines of Margaux.

Hôtel/Restaurant le Pont Bernet Ⓗ Ⓡ
Route du Verdon, Louens, 33290 le Pian Médoc. Tel 05 56 70 20 19; fax 05 56 70 22 90. Ⓕ Ⓕ
Modern rooms with swimming pool and tennis courts. Serves regional cuisine.

Restaurant le Savoie Ⓡ
33460 Margaux. Tel 05 57 88 31 76. Ⓕ Ⓕ
Excellent seasonal cuisine and extensive wine list, including a good selection of wines from Margaux AC.

Wines and Wine Villages

The allure of southern Médoc lies entirely in its fine wine-producing area close to the Gironde, in particular its history and the architecture and cellars of the great châteaux. The villages themselves are of passing interest. Even the flat landscape, with unbroken stretches of pine forest, offers little appeal, with the beach area to the west of the peninsula providing the main diversion.

Crus Classés   See p.21.

Haut-Médoc AC   The AC for the southern half of the Médoc peninsula, used for red wines only. It comprises the good vineyard land not already covered by the 6 communal ACs (Margaux, Moulis-en-Médoc, Listrac-Médoc, St-Julien, Pauillac and St-Estèphe) and appears in zones to the north and south of Margaux, west of St-Julien and Pauillac and west and north of St-Estèphe. The wine styles vary but are generally in the classic Médoc mould, being deep coloured, firm and concentrated.
Best producers: *Beaumont, Belgrave, le Bosq, Camensac, Cantemerle, Charmail, Cissac, Citran, Clément-Pichon, Coufran,* LA LAGUNE, LANESSAN, *Liversan, Malescasse, Maucamps, Moulin-Rouge, Sénéjac,* SOCIANDO-MALLET, *la Tour-Carnet,* TOUR-DU-HAUT-MOULIN, *Verdignan.*

Lamarque   Village with a small harbour, which operates a ferry service over to Blaye on the other side of the Gironde. Ch. de Lamarque is a wine estate with a castle dating from the Middle Ages, which was originally used as a defense against attacks from the estuary.

Listrac-Médoc AC   The small communal AC has varied soils, with zones of Garonne gravel, Pyrenean gravel, limestone and clay. The wines are accordingly varied: the classic Listrac style is firm and rather austere, but there are softer-edged wines produced using a higher percentage of Merlot. The co-operative, Grand-Listrac-la-Caravelle, is located in the centre of the village of Listrac-Médoc.

Best producers: *Cap-Léon-Veyrin,* CLARKE, *Ducluzeau, Fonréaud,* FOURCAS-DUPRÉ, *Fourcas-Hosten, Fourcas-Loubaney, Grand-Listrac-la Caravelle, Mayne-Lalande, Peyredon-Lagravette, Saransot-Dupré.*

Margaux AC   The village of Margaux is at the centre of the Margaux AC. It has a concentration of châteaux built in the 18th and 19th centuries, symbols of the newly acquired wealth of this epoque. The Maison du Vin is located on the northern edge of the village.

It is an important AC in the southern Médoc, with 1350ha of vineyards located in the communes of Arsac, Labarde, Cantenac, Margaux and Soussans. The AC has the highest percentage of the poor, gravelly soils found throughout the Médoc, which help produce intense, well-coloured wines of subtle, elegant flavour and aroma. There are 21 Crus Classés in Margaux, more than in any other AC.
Best producers: *d'Angludet, Brane-Cantenac, Cantenac-Brown, Dauzac, Durfort-Vivens, Ferrière, Giscours,* KIRWAN, LABÉGORCE-ZÉDÉ, *Lascombes, Malescot-St-Exupéry,* MARGAUX, *Marquis-de-Terne, Monbrison,* PALMER, PRIEURÉ-LICHINE, RAUZAN-SÉGLA, *Siran, du Tertre.*

Moulis-en-Médoc AC   The smallest of the Médoc's communal ACs takes its name from the village of Moulis. A Romanesque church with a beautifully engraved chancel is the only thing of interest here. Just outside the village there are a number of attractive watermills, including the Moulin de Tiquetorte.

The AC has only 570ha in vineyard production. The eastern sector around the village of Grand-Poujeaux has deep gravel soils and there is the potential here to produce great wines. Elsewhere, the wines are generally well made and represent excellent value, being lighter but vibrant with attractive fruit aromas.
Best producers: *Anthonic,* BISTON-BRILLETTE, *Brillette, Chasse-Spleen, Dutruch-Grand-Poujeaux, Gressier-Grand-Poujeaux, Malmaison,* MAUCAILLOU, POUJEAUX.

The long, narrow chai at Troisième Cru Ch. Palmer is stacked with first year oak barriques.

The domaine of Ch. Smith–Haut–Lafite in Pessac-Léognan AC consists of an uninterrupted block of 72ha, situated on a gravel hillock, of which 55ha are planted with vines. The gravel soils provide natural drainage, allowing the vine roots to penetrate to up to 6m (20ft) in search of water and mineral salts; the pebbles retain heat which helps to ripen the grapes. A system of 'rational protection of the vineyard' is employed; this includes the abandonment of the use of herbicides and limiting the use of fungicides. These practices are assisted by daily readings from an on-site meterological station. A new medieval-style reception room and balcony around the existing tower have now been added to the buildings seen here.

Ornate wrought-iron gates guard the vineyard of Ch. la Mission-Haut-Brion, source of powerful red wines for long aging.

Pessac-Léognan and Graves

Graves is one of the oldest viticultural zones in the Bordeaux region, and the vine has been cultivated around the city walls as far back as the Middle Ages. At that time under British sovereignty, its wines were known throughout the whole of northern Europe, and the 'new French claret' was drunk regularly in the taverns of London.

The region came to be known as the 'Grabas de Burdeus', or Graves de Bordeaux, because of the particular nature of its soils: deep, well-drained gravel ridges that provide exceptional conditions for grape-growing. Great red wines and limited quantities of white are produced in the northern Graves and Pessac-Léognan but, from further south where there is more sand, clay and limestone, there are some fruity reds and excellent dry whites – elegant Sauvignon/Sémillon-based wines that are often unknown or underestimated.

Bordeaux's urban expansion has gradually eaten into this vineyard area and continues to pose a threat today. The tour provides a memorable opportunity to tread these historic soils, now surrounded by the city sprawl, before heading south into a more rural setting.

The Tour

Leave the city centre of Bordeaux following signs for Pessac, exiting from the old town limits via the Barrière de Pessac. The road first winds through a residential and commercial district, but after about ten minutes the vines of Ch. la Mission-Haut-Brion appear on the left behind wrought-iron railings, bisected by the railway line from Bordeaux to Arcachon. The estate is under the same ownership and management as Ch. Haut-Brion, the firmly structured wines often rivalling those of its majestic stable mate.

On the right lies the vineyard of Ch. Haut-Brion, dominated by a water-tower, the 16th-century château and, in the distance, woods and high-rise office blocks. Despite its seemingly unpromising location, this is one of Bordeaux's great estates. In 1663 Samuel Pepys commented on the pleasure a certain 'Ho Bryan' had given him and, indeed, it was the only red wine outside the Médoc to be listed in the 1855 Classification. The pebble-strewn vineyard, planted on two knolls, is evidence of the *graves* epithet, and is one of the essential factors in producing these long-lived, minerally, Cabernet Sauvignon-dominated wines. Across the road, a small parcel of vines constitutes Ch. Laville-Haut-Brion, which produces an outstanding white Graves, albeit rarely.

TOUR SUMMARY

Starting from Bordeaux, the tour visits the historic châteaux of Pessac-Léognan, still within the confines of the city, before heading into the Graves countryside, ending in the village of Landiras.

Distance covered 110km (70 miles).

Time needed 7 hours.

Terrain The route meanders through urban sprawl to the west and south of the city, then heads out into the easy driving of the countryside. The twists and turns of the city roads can be misleading.

Hotels Although there are a few country options, the city of Bordeaux has a greater choice of hotels.

Restaurants There is a fair selection of places to eat in the region. The recommended restaurants offer regional dishes at value-for-money prices.

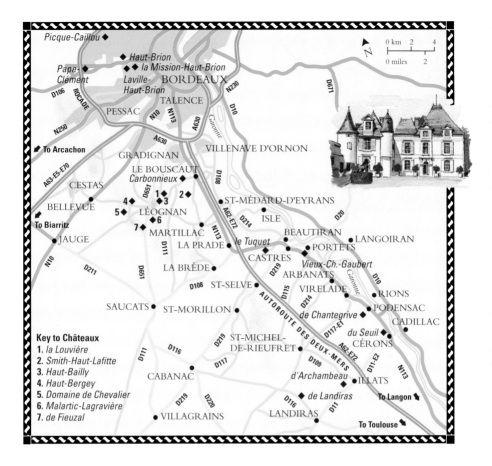

Map illustration: Ch. Haut-Brion.

A little further west in Pessac, not far from Bordeaux's busiest ring road, the Rocade, are the ivy-clad buildings and the park and vineyards of Ch. Pape-Clément. This is one of the oldest domaines in Bordeaux, taking the name from its most famous owner, Bertrand de Goth, who became Pope Clément V in 1305. The soils and the warm city meso-climate once more contribute to the excellence of the red wines. Due north of Pape-Clément, in a small verdant oasis, the last remaining property in Mérignac, Ch. Picque-Caillou, stands as a symbol against the creeping tide of urbanization. Surrounded on all sides by development, it is under constant pressure from projects linked to the expansion of nearby Mérignac airport. The wines are dry, firmly structured but slightly lean.

Time now to escape the city, so head south on the Rocade. Either exit at Gradignan for a meal at the Chalet Lyrique, or head directly for the little town of Léognan, an unexciting but pivotal point from which to visit the Crus Classés of the Graves. Bordeaux's sprawl begins to fade away and residential areas become interspersed with woods and meadows. At Léognan take the road for Cestas, passing the walls and gateway of Ch. Haut-Bergey. Under new ownership, this property has undergone a recent renaissance, and the brickwork of the turreted 18th-century building stands sparklingly clean, with brand new cellars to one side. The wines have also improved dramatically since 1994.

A road branches off to the left and continues through a dense, wooded area, suddenly breaking out into the open expanse of the Domaine de Chevalier vineyard. The entire estate is surrounded by forest, with a modern cellar complex along one edge. Chevalier is known for both its red and white wines, but the latter are particularly fine. These are made from predominantly Sauvignon Blanc, fermented and aged in new oak casks, which provides an intensity of citrus fruit flavours to match the lively acidity.

Continue in a circle toward the southern limits of Léognan to arrive at the new cellar complex of Ch. de Fieuzal, whose red wines have the density and mineral character of true Graves. The land here is more undulating, the soils strewn with white quartz pebbles, which again accentuate the *graves* terrain. Return to Léognan past Ch. Malartic-Lagravière, owned by the Champagne house Laurent-Perrier, and take the road past the cemetery toward le Bouscaut. Châteaux appear with great regularity, the majority reflecting the region's new-found prosperity, with open stretches of vineyard interspersed with pine forest.

Passing the good-value Haut-Bailly, the beautiful 18th-century listed château of la Louvière, home to some truly elegant reds and whites, and the walled property of Carbonnieux, turn down a wooded road toward

The sparkling new extension to the Domaine de Chevalier winery – shown here with owner Olivier Bernard – is another example of the progress being made in Pessac-Léognan AC.

Ch. Smith-Haut-Lafitte in the commune of Martillac. The vineyard is situated on a mound of gravel soil. Roses stand sentinel at the end of each row of vines and in their midst is a medieval-looking cellar complex, complete with balustrated tower. A little way off, an 18th-century Chartreuse stands shaded by trees. The property, which has its origins in the 14th century, is another that has undergone a revival in recent years. New cellars and a cooperage have contributed to the current excellence of both red and white wines.

Follow the N113 south into Graves AC toward Beautiran, where the land now becomes flatter, the vineyards interspersed with meadows and forest. An avenue lined with apple trees leads across the expanse of vineyards up to Ch. le Tuquet. The courtyard and farm buildings feel more approachable than the well-to-do estates in Pessac-Léognan, and the red wines are simple and honest, but still underpinned with Graves character.

Further down the road in Portets, Vieux-Château-Gaubert is demarcated by its clos (walled vineyard). The tasting room, standing in the ruins of the château, seems at first to be an unlikely roadside stop. In fact, this is a serious domaine which has been steadily replanted since 1988 and now makes good reds and barrel-fermented whites.

South toward Podensac the road runs parallel to the railway line and is shaded by plane trees. The flatness of the terrain on this side of the Garonne river is accentuated by the hills of the Premières Côtes de Bordeaux visible on the other side. The Maison des Vins de Graves in Podensac offers tastings and a good inventory of all the wines of the region for purchase. Lillet, an apéritif blend of the region's wines, citrus fruits and quinine, is also made in the village. Standing on the edge of Podensac, Ch. de Chantegrive, created from nothing in 1967, is now one of the top Graves properties. A little further south in Cérons, British owners Bob and Sue Watts are making attractive Graves wines at Ch. du Seuil.

Turn south-west toward Landiras. The road is first flanked by vineyards, then passes through forests and over the *autoroute* before crossing into the vineyards of Illats beyond. Ch. d'Archambeau is the top property in this commune. Ch. de Landiras is situated just outside the village of the same name, in the direction of Cabanac. The castle ruins date from the 14th century, the present château from the 19th century. Peter Vinding-Diers, one of the pioneers of the white Graves revolution, has reconstituted a vineyard that existed here in the 18th century. He makes an excellent barrel-fermented white wine essentially from Sémillon grapes. To complete the day, either return by *autoroute* to Bordeaux, or stay in the region for the Sweet Wine tour (see page 40).

The wines of the imposing Ch. la Louvière have improved steadily over the last 30 years.

Pessac-Léognan and Graves Fact File

Accommodation in the region is limited once outside the city of Bordeaux. Restaurants generally offer down to earth, regional fare at moderate prices. For a greater choice see Bordeaux City and Sweet Wine Fact Files (p.14 and p.44).

Information

Comité départemental du Tourisme
21 cours l'Intendance, 33000 Bordeaux. Tel 05 56 52 61 40; fax 05 56 81 09 99.

Maison des Vins de Graves
Route de Langon (N113), 33720 Podensac. Tel 05 56 27 09 25; fax 05 56 27 17 36.
The pamphlet *Les Graves accueillent* provides useful information for both Pessac-Léognan and Graves ACs. Wines are available to taste and buy, and there is an explanatory video in French of the Graves region. The building also houses the offices of the Syndicat Viticole des Graves et Graves Supérieures.

Syndicat Viticole de Pessac-Léognan
1 cours du XXX Juillet, 33000 Bordeaux. Tel 05 56 00 22 99; fax 05 56 48 53 79.

Union des Crus Classés de Graves
1 cours du XXX Juillet, 33000 Bordeaux. Tel 05 56 51 91 91; fax 05 56 51 64 12.

Markets
Pessac – Tuesday
Podensac – Tuesday and Friday

Festivals and Events
There are few festivals in the region. Pessac-Léognan has a Portes Ouvertes weekend in early December when visitors are welcomed for tastings without appointment. The wine brotherhood, the *Commanderie du Bontemps du Médoc et des Graves*, organizes a number of invitation-only events, including the *Fête de la Fleur* in June.

Where to Buy Wine
The châteaux of Pessac-Léognan do not generally sell their wines

The chai of Domaine de Chevalier is filled with new barrels for aging red wines and fermenting white.

direct to the public, but in the Graves, a number of estates offer cellar-door tastings and wines for purchase. Wines are available from the Maison des Vins de Graves (see above), but otherwise there are few wine shops. The city of Bordeaux offers a greater choice (see p.14).

Magnum Léognan
5 avenue Mal. de Lattre de Tassigny, 33850 Léognan. Comprehensive list of Graves wines and a selection from other Bordeaux ACs.

Where to Stay and Eat
Hotel/Restaurant le Chalet Lyrique Ⓗ Ⓡ
169 cours du Général-de-Gaulle, 33170 Gradignan. Tel 05 56 89 11 59; fax 05 56 89 53 37. Ⓕ Ⓕ
Restaurant with a reputation for its meat dishes, but there is also a good daily selection of fresh fish. The wine list has an adequate selection from Pessac-Léognan. The hotel has 40 comfortable, modern rooms.

Château de Balambis Ⓗ
RN113, 33640 Beautiran
Tel 05 56 67 51 29. Ⓕ Ⓕ
Country manor house offering bed and breakfast accommodation in 5 rooms.

The suite and bedroom in the tower are both spacious and well appointed.

Restaurant le Luma Ⓡ
RN113, 33640 Arbanats.
Tel 05 56 67 53 55. Ⓕ
In the Bordeaux region, *le luma* means a snail, but there is more than this on the menu at this establishment. A range of good, solid regional dishes is offered at moderate prices, and there is also a reasonable selection of local wines.

Restaurant la Maison de Cuisine Ⓡ
215 avenue des Pyrénées, 33140 Villenave d'Ornon. Tel 05 56 87 07 59. Ⓕ
Imaginative cuisine based on local produce and dishes, but with inspiration from the Mediterranean and elsewhere. The wine list features helpful comments from local wine producers. Good value.

Restaurant la Maison des Graves Ⓡ
Place de l'Église, 33650 la Brède. Tel 05 56 20 24 45. Ⓕ
Neat little restaurant in the centre of the village. *Alose*, or shad, is one of the house specialities. The wine list is accented toward the wines of the Graves, with some interesting discoveries.

Relais des Trois Mousquetaires Ⓡ
22 place Gambetta, 33720 Podensac. Tel 05 56 27 09 07. Ⓕ
Classic traditional family-run restaurant with good-value regional fare.

Hotel/Restaurant la Réserve Ⓗ Ⓡ
74 avenue Bourgailh, 33600 Pessac. Tel 05 56 07 13 28. fax 05 56 36 31 02. Ⓕ Ⓕ Ⓕ
The hotel offers peace and calm in its parkland setting. There are 22 spacious rooms, a swimming pool and other facilities. The restaurant features traditional cuisine with a number of set menus to choose from.

Wines and Wine Villages

The most southerly châteaux in Pessac-Léognan are no more than 15km (9 miles) from the centre of Bordeaux, so the city is a constant presence in the early part of the tour. The Graves is more scenic but the villages themselves are a little dull.

La Brède One of the Graves communes, la Brède delimits the northern part of the AC.

The writer and philosopher Charles Louis de Segondat, Baron de la Brède et de Montesquieu, was born here in 1689. The moated castle can be visited on most afternoons from April through to the beginning of November.

Crus Classés The Graves classification was inaugurated in 1953 and updated in 1959. It includes 13 red wines and 9 white wines. All the classified châteaux are located in Pessac-Léognan AC:
Bouscaut (red and white); Carbonnieux (red and white); Domaine de Chevalier (red and white); Couhins (white); Couhins-Lurton (white); de Fieuzal (red); Haut-Bailly (red); Haut-Brion (red); Laville-Haut-Brion (white); Malartic-Lagravière (red and white); la Mission-Haut-Brion (red); Olivier (red and white); Pape-Clément (red); Smith-Haut-Lafitte (red); la Tour-Haut-Brion (red); la Tour-Martillac (red and white).

Graves Supérieures AC
A dwindling AC reserved for semi-sweet and sweet white wines. There are still about 400ha in production.
Best producers: Clos St-Georges, Lehoul.

Graves AC An AC for red and dry whites that extends from la Brède in the north through to Mazères just south-east of Langon, enclosing Cérons, Sauternes and Barsac ACs. About 2000ha are planted with red grapes and 1000ha with white. Reds are produced from Cabernet Sauvignon and Merlot and have an attractive fruit and mineral character; the whites are made from Sémillon and

Sauvignon and are full, firm and bone-dry, with more intensity and elegance if they have been barrel fermented.
Best producers: d'Archambeau, d'Ardennes, le Bonnat, Brondelle, DE CHANTEGRIVE, *le Chec, Clos Floridène, la Grave, l'Hospital,* DE LANDIRAS, DE MALLE, *Magence, Magneau, Rahoul, Respide-Médeville, St-Robert, du Seuil,*

Portets' church is its main attraction, as well as the bizarre fountain with its oversized bunch of grapes.

LE TUQUET, VIEUX-CHÂTEAU-GAUBERT, *Villa-Bel-Air.*

Léognan An uninspiring village, but the most significant commune in Pessac-Léognan AC, in terms of the number of important châteaux that surround it.

Martillac The most southerly of the Pessac-Léognan communes. Ch. la Tour-Martillac, situated on the outskirts of the village, was at one time the property of the Baron de Montesquieu (see la Brède entry above).

Mérignac The airport is located in this suburb of

Bordeaux. It is also one of the Pessac-Léognan communes, but with only one château – Picque-Caillou – still in existence.

Pessac A suburb of Bordeaux that is home to Châteaux Haut-Brion and Pape-Clément.

Pessac-Léognan AC This AC, now consisting of some 1300ha of vines, was created in 1987. It covers the northern Graves and includes 10 communes located to the west and south of the city of Bordeaux. The soils are composed of deep, free-draining gravel – hence the origin of the name Graves de Bordeaux. The red wines are deeply coloured, full flavoured and textured, with Cabernet Sauvignon dominating the traditional Bordeaux blend. The whites, made from mostly Sauvignon (occasionally 100 per cent), are rich, aromatic and long-lived.
Best producers: Carbonnieux, les Carmes-Haut-Brion, DOMAINE DE CHEVALIER, *Couhins-Lurton,* DE FIEUZAL, *de France, la Garde, Haut-Bailly,* HAUT-BERGEY, HAUT-BRION, *Haut-Lagrange, Laville-Haut-Brion,* LA LOUVIÈRE, *Malartic-Lagravière, la Mission-Haut-Brion,* PAPE-CLÉMENT, *Picque-Caillou, de Rochemorin, le Sartre,* SMITH-HAUT-LAFITTE, *la Tour-Haut-Brion, la Tour-Martillac.*

Podensac This wine village in Graves AC has a lively market on Tuesday and Friday. The informative Maison des Vins de Graves is located here, as is the apéritif producer Lillet.

Portets The 19th-century Château de Portets is the most interesting feature of this wine village, although the church and the fountain in the central square are worth a look.

Talence The Bordeaux Institute of Enology is located in this suburb of the city, as are Châteaux la Mission-Haut-Brion and Laville-Haut-Brion.

The vineyard of Ch. d'Yquem is spread over a hillock at the highest point in Sauternes AC. The topsoil is a mixture of sand, gravel and clay, with a subsoil of clay and limestone in parts of the vineyard. The gravel and hillslopes provide good natural drainage but there is also a network of 100km (60 miles) of drainage pipes, installed in the 19th century. These features assist in the ripening of the grapes, but it is the autumnal morning mists produced by the cooler Ciron river flowing into the warmer Garonne that favour the development of *Botrytis cinerea* or noble rot, the requisite factor for producing the great sweet wines of Sauternes. Since this parasitic fungus does not spread in a uniform manner, a number of *tris*, or passes, through the vines must be made for selective hand-picking during the harvesting period.

Sweet Wines of Bordeaux

The 17th-century château of Premier Cru Ch. Suduiraut has grounds created by le Nôtre, the designer of the gardens at Versailles.

There is something special about the sweet white wines of Bordeaux, particularly those of Sauternes. It is not just a question of sweetness but also of richness and power, the complexity of aroma, intensity of flavour, and the ability of these wines to be appreciated young, or cellared for an indefinite time.

Sauternes and Barsac are, in fact, as much a triumph of nature as of man. In this southerly corner of Bordeaux, autumn mists are created by the cooler waters of the tiny Ciron river flowing into the warmer Garonne. This provides humid conditions ideal for the onset of *pourriture noble,* or noble rot (see page 9), caused by the fungus *Botrytis cinerea* – a phenomenon that further enriches the sugar content of the grapes. Sauternes and Barsac are two of the few regions in the world where this is a natural, although rare, occurrence. The wines are expensive – hardly surprising given the volatile climatic conditions, tiny yields and painstaking methods of production.

On the opposite bank of the Garonne river, the less well-known ACs of Cadillac, Loupiac and Ste-Croix-du-Mont also produce sweet wines from the same blend of Sémillon, Sauvignon and Muscadelle grapes. Here the conditions are less conducive to the onset of noble rot: its occurrence is more sporadic and the wines are lighter and less sweet, the product of the sun's rays rather than of 'rotten' grapes. The tour reveals the influencing factors of climate and geography in the wines' production, visiting some of the region's great estates along the way.

The Tour

The town of Langon is the starting point for the tour. Take the busy N113 to Preignac, then head south-west past the cemetery toward the village of Sauternes. The vineyards now come into view, compactly planted on fairly flat terrain.

Follow the signs, running first alongside then across the railway line, for Ch. de Malle, a property which offers historical, architectural and viticultural interest. The 17th-century château is open to the public and has a number of fine paintings and period pieces, and Italianate gardens. Although the wine is lighter in style than some of the more powerful Sauternes, it is fresh and aromatic and has also maintained the standards of its Cru Classé status.

Continue toward Sauternes, crossing the motorway and passing Ch. Bastor-Lamontagne, a large estate which makes one of Sauternes' more affordable wines. The land begins to

TOUR SUMMARY

A circular tour from Langon, visiting the attractive countryside of Sauternes and Barsac, before crossing the Garonne river to the friendly châteaux of the lesser-known ACs.

Distance covered   60km (38 miles).

Time needed   5 hours.

Terrain   The tour mainly uses the N113 and *départementale* roads that are easy to drive and to navigate. However, the network of tiny lanes in Barsac can be confusing.

Hotels   The choice of hotels in the countryside is quite limited. The city of Bordeaux offers a greater range of accommodation.

Restaurants   Quality restaurants in rural locations are few and far between, but there are a number of establishments providing simple regional fare at reasonable prices.

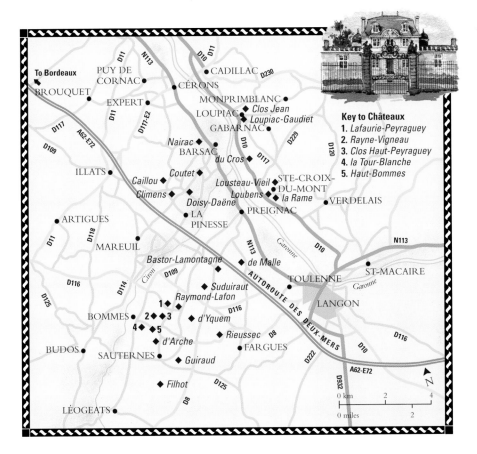

Map illustration: Ch. de Malle.

rise a little now, the vineyards becoming more clearly defined. The entrance to one of Sauternes' great estates, Ch. Suduiraut, looms to the right, partially obscured by a clump of trees. Behind the 17th-century château are beautiful gardens. The wines are rich and concentrated, in particular the special Cuvée Madame released in exceptional years.

On a knoll above Suduiraut, dominating the local vista, is the greatest sweet-wine producing estate in the world, Ch. d'Yquem. The top estates are all located on the higher ground of this rolling landscape, gaining better exposure to the sun and therefore greater ripeness and concentration in the grapes. This is clearly the case at Yquem, where selection of only botrytis-affected grapes, minuscule yields, and fermentation and aging in 100 per cent new oak barrels add to the distinction of the wine. The only estate to be classified Premier Cru Supérieur in 1855, Yquem continues to produce rich, powerful and long-lived wines. A visit to the cellars may be possible if arranged by correspondence well in advance of the trip. Otherwise, admire Yquem from a distance and continue heading south.

The road passes Ch. Rieussec, which dominates another hillock to the east of Yquem, and occasionally rivals it for power and concentration. Turning toward Sauternes, the vineyards remain uninterrupted, with the Crus Classés Chateaux Guiraud and Filhot clearly visible on either side of the road. The village of Sauternes itself is of interest mainly as a lunchtime stop and for information on the region – the Maison du Sauternes is located on the tiny village square. The restaurant le Saprien, opposite the tourist office on the rue Principal, is an innovative establishment; the Auberge les Vignes is more rustic.

Leaving Sauternes in the direction of Bommes, the road winds past an old wash-house and the Virginia-creeper-covered Ch. d'Arche. At Ch. Haut-Bommes turn left toward Bommes and Ch. la Tour-Blanche, a Premier Cru Classé owned by the French Ministry of Agriculture. The rugby pitch in front of the cellars is a reminder that la Tour-Blanche operates an agricultural college as well as producing wines. Since 1988 a number of changes, including vinification in 100 per cent new oak barrels, have led to a dramatic improvement in quality, and the wines, rich and exotic, are now among the best in the AC.

Below la Tour-Blanche the tiny village of Bommes is of interest primarily as a picnic spot. Follow directions for *les Bords du Ciron,* which lead to the banks of the tiny river Ciron. In fact, river is somewhat of an exaggeration, but the Ciron nevertheless makes its mark on the region, its cool waters a crucial element in the local mesoclimate, precipitating the autumn mists that promote noble rot.

Still in the commune of Bommes, heading back toward Preignac and Barsac, the road winds past Ch. Rayne-Vigneau and Ch. Clos Haut-Peyraguey, which is open for tastings. Ch. d'Yquem is now visible from another angle and there is a magnificent view over the surrounding countryside, with the steepled church of Ste-Croix-du-Mont visible in the distance.

At a crossroads sits Ch. Lafaurie-Peyraguey, part of which dates from the 13th century. Since the 1983 vintage, the wines of this attractive property have been absolutely sublime. Directly east, standing at the foot of Yquem's vineyards, is Ch. Raymond-Lafon. This estate, owned by Pierre Meslier the former manager of Ch. d'Yquem, was not included in the 1855 Classification, but produces wines every bit as powerful as the Crus Classés.

Following the road north again, the undulating countryside gives way to flatter terrain, with the vineyards finally petering out at a wooded copse. Head in the general direction of Barsac through woods and farmland, crossing the murky Ciron and its tributary and, finally, the motorway, to arrive in the vineyards of Barsac. The wines here have a lively acidity and are a little more delicate than those of Sauternes, although they can be labelled either Barsac or Sauternes. The terrain is lower lying than in Sauternes but,

Harvesting noble-rotted grapes – here, at Ch. d'Arche – is a labour-intensive process which contributes to the high cost of the wine.

being closer to the Garonne and Ciron rivers, often provides the right conditions for noble rot.

The roads here twist and turn in a spider's web of country lanes interspersed with tiny hamlets. The 18th-century manor house of Ch. Climens becomes prominent as the road winds toward Barsac. Although it is not obvious, the vineyard of this estate is located in the highest part of the commune. The wines have long been considered the best in Barsac, with great length and finesse but greater delicacy than the more powerful Sauternes. North of Climens Jean-Bernard Bravo provides a warm welcome to visitors at the more obscure but competent Ch. Caillou. Excellent wines are also made at nearby Châteaux Doisy-Daëne and Coutet.

Now head to the village of Barsac. In the centre, the Maison de Barsac is open for tastings and the purchase of wines. On the northern edge of the village, Ch. Nairac offers a last chance to taste at one of the AC's finer properties. The vineyard and cellars date from 1610, but the château was built by a Huguenot négociant from Bordeaux in 1786. The wines have a rich, concentrated, oaky character.

The road north from Barsac is shaded by an alley of plane trees. At the sweet wine village of Cérons turn toward Cadillac, crossing to the right bank of the Garonne river. The *bastide*, or fortified village, of Cadillac stands on the river's edge. The impressive 17th-century Ch. des Ducs d'Epernon is worth a visit, if only to taste the rather light-weight sweet wines of Cadillac at the Maison du Vin located within the château.

Out of Cadillac follow the signs back toward Langon. The road runs parallel to the Garonne, with vineyards planted on the slopes to the north-east. Climb through the village and vineyards of Loupiac to Clos Jean, located in the undulating countryside above. The property was originally a staging post on the pilgrim route to Santiago de Compostela. The wines here are as rich and concentrated as any in the AC and in exceptional years, such as 1990 and 1995, approach the intensity of a decent Sauternes or Barsac.

Either follow the back lanes from Clos Jean or return to the D10, passing Châteaux Loupiac-Gaudiet and du Cros, two other admirable properties in Loupiac, before turning off the road and climbing up to Ste-Croix-du-Mont. From the church square there is a magnificent view over the Garonne Valley. The vineyards of Ch. Lousteau-Vieil are located on clay-limestone soils at 118m (390ft), the highest point in the commune. With a large percentage of Muscadelle in the blend, the wines are always fresh, fruity and aromatic. Châteaux la Rame and Loubens also make fine wines. Finally, return to Langon, perhaps stopping off in Verdelais, where the painter Toulouse-Lautrec is buried.

The village of Ste-Croix-du-Mont is at the centre of the best AC for mildly sweet wines on the right bank of the Garonne river.

Sweet Wines Fact File

Langon is the only major town in the region. The choice of hotels and restaurants is limited – see Pessac-Léognan and Graves Fact File (p.36) and Entre-Deux-Mers Fact File (p.52) for further options. The pamphlet *Découverte Sauternes & Barsac*, available from the Offices du Tourisme and Maisons du Vin, provides useful information for visiting the châteaux.

Information

Maison du Sauternes
33210 Sauternes. Tel. 05 56 76 69 83; fax 05 56 76 69 67.
Stocks a reasonable selection of wines which are available for tasting and purchase.

Office du Tourisme
Allée Jean Jaurès, 33210 Langon. Tel 05 56 62 34 00; fax 05 56 63 43 81.
Pick up the *Découverte Sauternes & Barsac* guide here.

Office du Tourisme
33210 Sauternes. Tel 05 56 76 69 13; fax 05 56 76 69 67.

Syndicat Viticole de Barsac
and the **Maison de Barsac**
33720 Barsac. Tel 05 56 27 08 73; fax 05 56 27 03 71.
A selection of wines is available for tasting and purchase.

Syndicat Viticole de Cérons
BP11, 33720 Cérons. Tel 05 56 27 01 13; fax 05 56 27 22 17.

Syndicat Viticole de Loupiac
Domaine du Noble, 33410 Loupiac. Tel 05 56 62 98 30; fax 05 56 76 91 31.

Syndicat Viticole Premières Côtes de Bordeaux Blancs & Cadillac
BP10, 33410 Cadillac. Tel 05 56 62 67 18; fax 05 56 62 19 82.

Syndicat Viticole de Ste-Croix-du-Mont
Ch. Loubens, 33410 Ste-Croix-du-Mont. Tel 05 56 62 01 25; fax 05 56 76 71 65.

Syndicat Viticole de Sauternes
Place de la Mairie, 33410 Sauternes. Tel 05 56 76 60 37; fax 05 56 76 69 67.

Markets

Barsac – Sunday
Cadillac – Saturday
Langon – Friday

Festivals and Events

Sauternes and Barsac operate a Portes Ouvertes weekend in June when the châteaux issue an open invitation for visits and tastings. In September the *Fête du Soleil* celebrates the coming

A useful source of information, the Maison du Sauternes also offers wines of the region to taste and buy.

vintage; a different château hosts the event each year. There is a wine, cheese and bread festival which is held in Langon, also in September. These events are all open to the public.

Where to Buy Wine

Local wines are available at the Maisons du Vin and direct from most properties. The great estates of Sauternes and Barsac often have a limited list of wines for sale, including older vintages. There are few wine shops in the region.

Le Cellier des Chanoines
33410 Cadillac.
Small selection of local wines. Café-bar attached.

Where to Stay and Eat

Restaurant le Cap (R)
Bords de Garonne, 33210 Preignac. Tel 05 56 63 27 38. (F)
Simple bistro on the banks of the

Garonne, serving standard regional dishes.

Hôtel/Restaurant Château de la Tour (H)(R)
33410 Cadillac-Beguey. Tel 05 56 76 92 00; fax 05 56 62 11 59. (F)(F)
Modern establishment overlooking the Château des Ducs d'Epernon, with swimming pool, fitness centre and terrace. Comfortable rooms and a restaurant serving well-prepared regional dishes.

Hôtel Château de Valmont (H)
33720 Barsac. Tel 05 56 27 28 24; fax 05 56 27 17 53. (F)(F)
A quiet retreat in the village of Barsac. There are 12 well-appointed rooms in the 18th-century building. Restaurant for residents only.

Hôtel/Restaurant Claude Darroze (H)(R)
95 cours du Général Leclerc, 33210 Langon. Tel 05 56 63 00 48; fax 05 56 63 41 15. (F)(F)(F)
Legendary establishment in the centre of Langon. Restaurant provides classic cuisine and an extensive wine list. A variety of game dishes are served in season. Ten rooms.

Restaurant le Saprien (R)
33210 Sauternes. Tel 05 56 76 60 87; fax 05 56 76 68 92. (F)(F)
Imaginative regional dishes and comprehensive wine list. Terrace overlooking the vines for summer dining.

Restaurant la Table du Sauternais (R)
Lieu-dit Boutoc, 33210 Preignac. Tel 05 56 63 43 44. (F)
Simple country restaurant in the centre of the Sauternes region. Seasonal dishes.

Auberge les Vignes (R)
33210 Sauternes. Tel 05 56 76 60 06. (F)
Local products and homemade food served in a rustic setting. Try the *entrecôte à la Bordelaise* (steak cooked over vine cuttings) and the pastries. Good wine list.

Wines and Wine Villages

The interest in the sweet wine region lies principally in the châteaux and countryside. The villages themselves are a little dull, with the exception of Cadillac.

Barsac AC   Along with Sauternes this is the most important sweet white wine AC in Bordeaux. The best properties are south-west of the town on the slightly higher Haut-Barsac plateau. Châteaux have the right to label their wines either Barsac or Sauternes. Compared to Sauternes, the wines are usually more delicate with a crisp acidity, perhaps due to the greater percentage of limestone and sand in the soils.
Best producers: Cru Barrejats, Broustet, Caillou, CLIMENS, Coutet, Doisy-Daëne, Doisy-Dubroca, Doisy-Védrines, Gravas, de Myrat, NAIRAC, Piada, Roumieu-Lacoste, Suau.

Bommes   A quiet backwater located on the tiny Ciron river and one of the 5 Sauternes communes.

Cadillac AC   Tiny AC for sweet wines, centred on the lively village of the same name. Until 1973 it was part of the Premières Côtes de Bordeaux. The wines are not expensive, but rarely reach the quality levels of neighbouring Loupiac and Ste-Croix-du-Mont.
Best producers: Fayau, Peyruchet.

Cérons AC   An AC for sweet white wines just north of Barsac and Sauternes. Size and low prices prevent investment in quality, but there are some good examples.
Best producers: de Cérons, Grand Enclos du Château de Cérons.

Crus Classés   Sauternes and Barsac were also included in the 1855 Classification of the Médoc, the evaluation once again based on the price fetched by the sweet wines. Ch. d'Yquem has its own rank, which is higher than any of the Premier Cru red wines; in addition, there are 11 Premiers Crus and 12 Deuxièmes Crus:

Premier Cru Supérieur: Yquem.
Premiers Crus: Climens, Coutet, Guiraud, Clos Haut-Peyraguey, Lafaurie-Peyraguey, Rabaud-Promis, Rayne-Vigneau, Rieussec, Sigalas-Rabaud, Suduirat, la Tour-Blanche.
Deuxièmes Crus: d'Arche, Broustet, Caillou, Doisy-Daëne, Doisy-Dubroca, Doisy-Védrines, Filhot, Lamothe, Lamothe-Guignard, de Myrat, Nairac, Romer-du-Hayot, Suau, de Malle.

Wines from Barsac AC can be labelled either Barsac or Sauternes.

Fargues   One of the 5 Sauternes communes, but of little interest except to view the château ruins from a distance.

Langon   An administrative centre on the banks of the Garonne and locally the most important town.

Loupiac AC   The village between Cadillac and Ste-Croix-du-Mont gives its name to the AC. The vineyards overlook the Garonne and, in the better vintages, the onset of noble rot gives greater concentration to otherwise light, medium-sweet wines. They are often excellent value for money.
Best producers: du Chay, CLOS JEAN, du Cros, Loupiac-Gaudiet, du Noble, Mazarin.

Preignac   One of the Sauternes communes. The village itself has an impressive 18th-century church with cupola.

Ste-Croix-du-Mont AC   The best of the sweet white wine ACs on the right bank of the Garonne. The village of the same name has an impressive view out over the Garonne Valley. Underneath Ch. de Ste-Croix-du-Mont are a number of caves full of fossilized oysters which can be visited.

The vineyards are planted on clay-limestone soils, parts of which have a gravel topsoil, and there is the potential for noble rot to develop. Some producers ferment and age their wines in barrel. The top wines can be a better deal than some of the more lowly Sauternes.
Best producers: Crabitan-Bellevue, Laurette, Loubens, LOUSTEAU-VIEIL, du Mont, la Rame.

Sauternes AC   Including Barsac, the AC constitutes some 2200ha of vineyards. Botrytis-affected grapes produce rich, opulent, powerful wines with a minimim alcohol strength of 13 per cent. A cocktail of fruit aromas and honeyed texture is the norm in youth, evolving to dried fruits and roasted nuts with age. The best Sauternes can age for 50 years or more.
Best producers: d'Arche, Bastor-Lamontagne, CLOS HAUT-PEYRAGUEY, de Fargues, Gilette, Guiraud, Haut-Bergeron, les Justices, LAFAURIE-PEYRAGUEY, Lamothe, Lamothe-Guignard, DE MALLE, Rabaud-Promis, Rayne-Vigneau, RIEUSSEC, St-Amand, Sigalas-Rabaud, SUDUIRAUT, LA TOUR-BLANCHE, YQUEM.

The Moulin du Haut-Benauge, set amid the vineyards near Gornac in the rolling countryside of Entre-Deux-Mers, indicates the region's former importance as a cereal-growing area. Haut-Benauge AC, officially approved in 1955, is delimited by nine communes in the region, including those of Targon and Gornac. Red wines account for 60 per cent of production in the Entre-Deux-Mers, and can only be declared under the Bordeaux and Bordeaux Supérieur ACs. Entre-Deux-Mers Haut-Benauge is the designation for dry white wines, and Bordeaux Haut-Benauge for dry and sweet whites. Production of the latter is minuscule – only a handful of winemakers still use the traditional methods needed to qualify for the designation.

The Garonne river is a constant presence in the Entre-Deux Mers region, being one of the two 'seas' that gives the region its name.

Entre-Deux-Mers

There are no Cru Classé châteaux in the Entre-Deux-Mers but don't let that deter anyone from visiting the region. The wines here, both red and white, have a fresh, wholesome, down-to-earth character and are made for instant pleasure at affordable prices – a case of decent wine here often costs much the same as a single bottle from one of the more lofty châteaux. The revolution in efficient wine-making has also passed this way, and quality has risen considerably recently, not just at small domaines but at the co-operatives, which play an important role in the region. Add to this the fact that producers are happy to receive visitors, and that the countryside contains a treasure trove of medieval castles, abbeys and fortified villages, and there are more than enough reasons for a visit.

The Entre-Deux-Mers is the wedge of land that lies between the Garonne and Dordogne rivers (hence its name). It includes the ACs Entre-Deux-Mers (for white wines only), Bordeaux and Bordeaux Supérieur for basic wines, Prèmieres Côtes de Bordeaux and the little-known Graves de Vayres, Côtes de Bordeaux St-Macaire, Ste-Foy-Bordeaux and Haut-Benauge. Given the extent of the region, some 2400 sq. km (1000 sq. miles), the tour does not attempt to touch base with all these, but instead highlights the dynamism being shown by certain ACs and individuals, at the same time exploring the beauty of the countryside.

The Tour

Leaving the city of Bordeaux via the new Pont d'Arcins in the direction of Paris, take the exit for Bouliac, a tiny village in the northern part of the Premières Côtes de Bordeaux. Blessed with an eclectic selection of restaurants, Bouliac's hilltop position also affords a panoramic view back over the Garonne to the city of Bordeaux beyond.

The road (D10) follows the meandering course of the Garonne upstream in a south-easterly direction. On the river side of the road the land is flat and silty, vineyards alternating with cereal crops; the wines produced here are entitled only to the ACs Bordeaux or Bordeaux Supérieur. On the other side, 18th- and 19th-century manor houses are dotted along wooded slopes that rise to the top of a limestone scarp. The vineyards of the Premières Côtes de Bordeaux are situated on this south-east-facing calcareous bluff, as well as around the series of twisting hills and valleys behind.

The charm and potential of the Premières Côtes have drawn a number of would-be winegrowers to the region over recent years, giving new vigour to the AC. Turn up any of the little valley roads on the left and you are almost

TOUR SUMMARY

A circular tour of this large region, starting in the city of Bordeaux, and crossing the Garonne river into the beautiful rolling countryside around the towns of St-Macaire and Sauveterre-de-Guyenne.

Distance covered 150km (95 miles).

Time needed 7 hours.

Terrain Away from Bordeaux the tour winds along *départementale* routes and smaller country roads that are slow-moving but easy to follow.

Where to stay The city of Bordeaux is the main choice for a wide range of accommodation; otherwise there are some simple hotels in the key towns and in the countryside.

Where to eat There are plenty of simple inns with inexpensive fixed-price menus. For more adventurous cuisine, head for the periphery of the city of Bordeaux.

To Paris · BEYCHAC-ET-CAILLAU · To St-Émilion · N89-E70 · D13 · N89 · D670 · N

0 km   4   8
0 miles   4

BORDEAUX

CASTILLON-LA-BATAILLE

N230 · D936 · Dordogne · ST-PEY-DE-CASTETS

A2630 · BOULIAC · D10 · GRÉZILLAC · Gamage ◆ ●

DAIGNAC · D670 · D121 · PUJOLS

● LATRESNE · Bonnet · D128 · de Courteillac ◆ · D17

CAMBLANES · CRÉON · D239 · D11 · RAUZAN · RUCH

D671 · Thieuley ◆ · LA SAUVE-MAJEURE · D127E

● QUINSAC · D239

Garonne · ◆ Puy-Bardens · ◆ Lamothe-de-Haux · BELLEBAT · BLASIMON

A62-E72 · ● CAMBES · HAUX · TARGON · D671 · D129

N113 · D20 · LANGOIRAN · D237 · D17

PORTETS · D10 · D119 · HAUT-LANGOIRAN · ST-BRICE · To St-Ferme

AUTOROUTE DES DEUX-MERS · Langoiran · COIRAC · SAUVETERRE-DE-GUYENNE · D230

RIONS ● · ◆ Carsin · D11 · D228 · GORNAC ●

CÉRONS · ◆ Reynon · ● CADILLAC · D230 · D672 · D670

D131 · ST-ANDRÉ-DU-BOIS

Malromé ◆ · ● GIRONDE-SUR-DROPT · LA RÉOLE

A62-E72 · N113 · D10 · ST-MAIXANT · N113

To Toulouse · ● ST-MACAIRE · Garonne · To Marmande

Map illustration: vineyard scene in the Entre-Deux-Mers.

certain to find a motivated and well-run family-owned domaine. At Cambes, where the village runs down to the edge of the sleepy Garonne, a country lane climbs up to Ch. Puy-Bardens, whose château and cellars stand on a hillock, with vineyards running away on all sides down to the forested valley floor below. The Lamiable family, Champenois of origin, arrived here ten years ago and have developed the vineyards, modernized the cellars and introduced barrel-aging and a second label, all to good effect.

Further along the river, in the hinterland near the village of Haux, is another hilltop château, that of Ch. Lamothe-de-Haux. The limestone nature of the region is witnessed in the stone used to construct the 18th-century château, and in the cellars created from the resulting underground quarries. As elsewhere in the Premières Côtes, the red wines of Lamothe-de-Haux are made from a blend of Merlot and Cabernet and have an attractive freshness and fruit character.

Back down toward the river, at the 12th-century Ch. Langoiran, wines of the same name are produced just below the castle ruins. Francis Neeser, originally a farmer from the Marne, has profited from the existence of ancient cellars for barrel-aging his wines, but he has also modernized the domaine by installing stainless steel tanks and harvesting by machine, now a common cost-effective development throughout the Entre-Deux-Mers region. From here, there is a splendid view that takes in the vineyards of the surrounding Premières Côtes and the flood plain of the Garonne.

As the road heads south-east toward Rions, the hills begin to fan out a little and the vineyards are dotted with rows of poplar trees and, curiously, the occasional parasol pine. Rions is a fortified village whose 14th-century walls are redolent of medieval pageantry. Above, in the hills of the Premières Côtes, the modern era has also been embraced at Ch. Carsin. Finnish owner Juha Berglund has installed state-of-the-art equipment and employed the services of an Australian winemaker to make the best of his terroir. Down the road at Ch. Reynon, Professor Denis Dubordieu of Bordeaux's Institute of Enology produces excellent white Bordeaux and red Premières Côtes.

From here continue south to the medieval village of St-Macaire, before heading north on the D672 toward Sauveterre-de-Guyenne. Stop off to visit Ch. Malromé, the family home and summer retreat of the painter Toulouse-Lautrec; the estate now produces a creditable Bordeaux Supérieur, which you can try in the tasting room. Head along the D131 road, turning right toward Gornac. The road to Sauveterre runs over a high, rolling plateau of vineyards, arable farmland and forest, passing the Moulin du Haut-Benauge and the village of Coirac, which is garlanded in flowers in the spring and summer.

Harvesting by machine – here, at Sauveterre-de-Guyenne – is one of several technological improvements taking place in the Entre-Deux-Mers.

Sauveterre itself is an agreeable 13th-century *bastide*, or fortified village – a pleasant spot to break the journey. The local co-operative, Cellier de la Bastide, has a progressive outlook and a reputation for the quality of its dry white wines, produced in both Bordeaux AC and Entre-Deux-Mers AC. Sauvignon Blanc, in particular, has been set at a premium, and there are now a number of Cuvées made entirely from this variety.

The D17 road north from Sauveterre dips down into a valley, the vineyards temporarily replaced by meadow and trees. Passing the ruins of the 12th-century abbey at Blasimon, climb back up to the plateau near Ruch. A country lane turns into a dirt track, which bumps and twists down to Domaine de Courteillac, owned by Stéphane Asseo, one of Bordeaux's go-ahead young winemakers. He bought the property in 1982 in such a rundown state that there was no electricity or water and cattle were sheltering in the *chai*. He has since replanted 10ha of vineyard and renovated the cellars, and now produces a very good barrel-aged Bordeaux Supérieur. Further north at St-Pey-de-Castets, Ch. Gamage makes a pleasant visit, producing attractive red Bordeaux and white Entre-Deux-Mers wines.

Head west to Rauzan, with its ruined fortress, to visit the Union des Producteurs de Rauzan, the largest co-operative producer of AC wines in France. Membership covers 2100ha of vineyard land producing an annual average total of 120,000 hectolitres of wine. The figures are monstrous but quality levels are good given the volume of production, helped by a steady programme of investment in equipment and technology and improved grape-growing.

North-west from Rauzan the route D128 meanders through tiny tree-lined valleys and vine-clad hills. One of the early pioneers of improvement in the region, André Lurton, lives and directs his large viticultural empire from Ch. Bonnet (he also owns Châteaux la Louvière and Couhins-Lurton in Pessac-Léognan), not far from the village of Grézillac. Inheriting the 18th-century château and 30ha of vineyard in 1942, he has since expanded this to 225ha and has developed a range of wines that are notable for their consistency. The Ch. Bonnet Entre-Deux-Mers, in particular, is typical of the new order of crisp, fresh, fruity white examples now found in the region.

Turning south-west, the D239 dips through a small stretch of forest, reappearing at the abbey of la Sauve-Majeure. Just beyond, in the direction of Créon, Francis Courselle at Ch. Thieuley is another forward-thinking character who, over the last 25 years, has replanted the vineyards, restructured the cellars and invested in modern equipment. The result has once again been consistent quality in both white and red wines, the latter aged in a mix of oak barrels and larger vats.

Before returning to Bordeaux or stopping for a well-earned meal in Bouliac, head north to Beychac-et-Caillau to pay a visit to the Maison de Qualité, the shop window for the Bordeaux and Bordeaux Supérieur ACs, where there is a selection of over 800 wines at cellar-door prices.

The superb ruined fortress at Rauzan dominates the town, which is also home to the largest co-operative producer of AC wines in France.

Entre-Deux-Mers Fact File

There is a host of things to see and do in the area. Regional tourist offices have plenty of documentary information. The booklet *Balades en Premières Côtes de Bordeaux*, available from the offices of the Syndicat, is useful for visiting both the châteaux and historical monuments of the region. There are any number of small local restaurants offering regional food, but good hotels are a little thinner on the ground. For a greater choice of hotels and restaurants, check the Sweet Wines of Bordeaux and the City of Bordeaux Fact Files (p.44 and p.14).

Information

Maison de la Qualité
N89, 33750 Beychac-et-Caillau. Tel 05 56 72 90 99; fax 05 56 72 81 02.
Shop window for Bordeaux and Bordeaux Supérieur ACs, with a list of names and addresses of producers whose wines it stocks. (Reopening spring 1998 following a major extension.)

Office du Tourisme
7 bis rue du Docteur Fauché, 33670 Créon. Tel 05 56 68 54 41; fax 05 56 68 56 74.

Office du Tourisme
4 place du Docteur Abant, 33550 Langoiran. Tel 05 56 67 56 18; fax 05 56 67 56 74.

Office du Tourisme
2 rue St-Romain, 33540 Sauveterre-de-Guyenne. Tel 05 56 71 53 45; fax 05 56 71 59 39.

Syndicat Viticole de l'Entre-Deux-Mers
33670 la Sauve-Majeure. Tel 05 57 34 32 12.
Stocks the booklet *Balades en Premières Côtes de Bordeaux*.

Syndicat Viticole des Premières Côtes de Bordeaux (Rouge)
Place de l'Église, 33360 Quinsac. Tel 05 56 20 85 84; fax 05 56 20 88 63.

Markets

Créon – Wednesday
Langoiran – Thursday
Rauzan – Saturday
La Réole – Saturday
Sauveterre-de-Guyenne – Tuesday

Festivals and Events

The Premières Côtes de Bordeaux welcomes visitors during a Portes Ouvertes weekend in May (accompanied by a procession of vintage cars), as do châteaux in Bordeaux AC and Bordeaux Supérieurs AC during the first weekend in October.

Modern equipment at the Rauzan co-operative, such as these fermentation tanks, helps produce consistent wines.

Where to Buy Wine

This is a region in which producers are happy to sell direct to the public, so allow plenty of space in your car. There are few wine shops.

La Vinothèque
4 place de la République, 33540 Sauveterre-de-Guyenne. Tel 05 56 71 61 28; fax 05 56 71 59 39.
A selection of wines from the local district.

Where to Stay and Eat

Restaurant de l'Abbaye Ⓡ
Place de la Mairie, 33670 La Sauve-Majeure. Tel 05 56 23 21 58. Ⓕ
Unpretentious restaurant serving simple regional fare alongside local wines.

Restaurant l'Abricotier Ⓡ
33490 St-Macaire. Tel 05 56 76 83 63; fax 05 56 76 28 51. Ⓕ Ⓕ
Restaurant with attractive modern décor offering contemporary regional cuisine. There is a garden terrace for summer dining.

Restaurant le Bistroy Ⓡ
33270 Bouliac. Tel 05 57 97 06 06; fax 05 56 20 92 58. Ⓕ
Excellent bistro cuisine prepared in the kitchens of the Hotel St-James (see p.53). Local wines featured. Some tables are in the conservatory, which can become hot on sunny days.

Restaurant le Café de l'Espérance Ⓡ
33270 Bouliac. Tel 05 56 20 52 16. Ⓕ
Back-to-basics restaurant, serving grilled meats and other tasty regional food.

Auberge de la Chapelle Ⓡ
Place de la Chapelle, 33550 Langoiran. Tel 05 56 67 26 27. Ⓕ
Discrete little restaurant serving regional dishes. A fair selection of Premières Côtes on the adequate wine list.

Hostellerie du Château Lardier Ⓗ Ⓡ
33350 Ruch. Tel 05 57 40 54 11; fax 05 57 40 70 38. Ⓕ Ⓕ
Quiet country retreat in the middle of the vineyards, with 10 well-kept rooms. There is a choice of fixed-price menus and wines from the estate.

Château du Parc Ⓗ
33580 St-Ferme. Tel 05 56 61 69 18. Ⓕ Ⓕ
Bed and breakfast is offered in this tranquil 18th-century château, which stands in its own parkland. Five bedrooms and 2 suites available. Dinner is based on local seasonal produce and is available to residents if booked in advance.

Restaurant le Flore ®
33540 Coirac. Tel 05 56 71 57
47. Ⓕ
Honest cuisine from a fairly new
restaurant housed in a renovated
country house. The wine list
is limited.

**Restaurant la Maison du
Fleuve ®**
Port Neuf, 33360 Camblanes.
Tel 05 56 20 06 40. Ⓕ Ⓕ
Riverside restaurant built of
wood. Fresh, lively cuisine with
fish dishes the speciality. Well-
selected wine list.

Auberge du Marais ®
22 route de Latresne, 33270
Bouliac. Tel 05 56 20 52 17;
fax 05 56 20 98 06. Ⓕ Ⓕ
Classic restaurant with fresh fish
dishes and *canard à l'orange* the
specialities.

**Hôtel/Restaurant les Trois
Cèdres Ⓗ ®**
33190 Gironde-sur-Dropt.
Tel 05 56 71 10 70; fax 05 56 71
12 10. Ⓕ Ⓕ
Traditional cuisine with seasonal
dishes, including *cèpe* mushrooms
and *entrecôte*, served on the terrace

under the trees. 10 rooms. Small
list of local wines.

**Hôtel/Restaurant
St-James Ⓗ ®**
33270 Bouliac. Tel 05 57 97 06
00; fax 05 56 20 92 58. Ⓕ Ⓕ Ⓕ
Modern, luxury hotel with
rooms overlooking the city of
Bordeaux. The restaurant, one
of the best in the region, offers
very good, inventive cuisine.
Spiced grilled pigeon is one of
the classics. Fixed price menus,
as well as à la carte, and an
extensive wine list.

Wines and Wine Villages

Almost without exception the villages and towns in the
Entre-Deux-Mers have some historical or architectural
interest. Medieval history, in particular, is strongly
represented in the region. Wine is part of the local culture
and economy, so the villages are all 'wine villages' but in a
more low-key fashion than in the more famous ACs. The
co-operatives play an important role throughout the
Entre-Deux-Mers.

Blasimon   Tiny *bastide*, or
fortified village, with the
interesting ruins of a late 12th-
century abbey on its outskirts.
There is an important
co-operative, les Vignerons
de Guyenne, and an outdoor
recreation area, which has
provisions for picnicking.

Bordeaux AC and **Bordeaux
Supérieur AC**   Bordeaux AC
is the basic generic AC for wines
produced in any part of the
Bordeaux region. It applies to
red, dry and sweet white and
rosé wines. Bordeaux Supérieur
AC applies to the same area, but
the wines must have a higher
minimum percentage of alcohol
and must be produced from
lower yields. Red wines
produced in the Entre-Deux-
Mers zone take either the
Bordeaux AC or Bordeaux
Supérieur AC.
Best producers: BONNET, *Cazeau,*
DE COURTEILLAC, *la France,*
Gamage, le Grand-Verdus,
de Reignac, Reynon, Roquefort,
de Seguin, de Sours, THIEULEY,
Trocard, Turon-la-Croix.

**Côtes de Bordeaux-St-
Macaire AC**   Rarely used AC
for semi-sweet white wines near
the attractive medieval village of
St-Macaire.

Entre-Deux-Mers AC   For
dry white wines produced in a
crisp, fresh, fruity fashion from a
blend of Sauvignon, Sémillon
and Muscadelle. The AC has
been the scene of a recent
wine-making revolution, with
improved control of vine diseases
and stricter selection of grapes
as well as investment in stainless
steel tanks and systems of
temperature control.
Best producers: BONNET,
Castelneau, CELLIER DE LA
BASTIDE, *Launay, Nardique-la-
Gravière, Ste-Marie, Turcaud.*

**Premières Côtes de Bordeaux
AC**   AC for red and sweet
white wines, covering an area
that runs parallel to the Garonne
river for 60km (35 miles) from
just south of Bordeaux to St-
Maixant. The reds, made from a
blend of Merlot and Cabernet,
are produced mainly in the

northern half of the AC; the
whites from Sémillon and
Sauvignon are from vineyards
centred on Cadillac further
south. Dry white wines are sold
under Bordeaux AC.
Best producers: (red) *Brethous,*
CARSIN, *Chelivette, Constantin,*
Haux, Jonchet, LAMOTHE-DE-
HAUX, LANGOIRAN, *Melin,*
PUY-BARDENS, *Reynon, Sauvage,*
le Sens, Suau, Tanesse.

Rauzan   Site of a superb
fortress and home to the large
co-operative, Union des
Producteurs de Rauzan.

St-André-du-Bois   Although
the village itself has little to offer,
Ch. Malromé is worth a visit.
Once the summer retreat and
family home of the painter
Toulouse-Lautrec, it is now a
working wine estate. Toulouse-
Lautrec is buried in the cemetery
at Verdelais close by.

St-Macaire   Medieval village
with some 13th-century houses
visible and a ring of fortified
gateways still in existence. The
village gives its name to a tiny AC.
See also **Côtes de Bordeaux-
St-Macaire AC**.

Sauveterre-de-Guyenne   The
four original gateways of this
attractive 13th-century *bastide*, or
fortified village, still remain
intact. The local co-operative, le
Cellier de la Bastide, is noted for
its white wines.

The tiny 7ha Ch. Ausone in St-Émilion AC is located on the edge of the town of St-Émilion. The south–south–easterly exposure of the vineyards, planted mainly on the steep, southern slopes of St-Émilion, provide an ideal mesoclimate for the ripening of the grapes. The extremely poor soils are a mix of limestone, clay and *molasse* (sedimentary rock), providing good drainage and an added complexity in the wines. The vines are, on average, 35 years old. The grapes, 50 per cent Merlot and 50 per cent Cabernet Franc, are picked and vinified in oak vats according to each individual parcel of land.

Located right on the border with Pomerol, Ch. Cheval-Blanc is considered to be one of the top estates of St-Émilion.

St-Émilion

There are any number of good reasons for visiting St-Émilion and its adjacent communes. The rolling countryside is at its most picturesque and, historically, there is much to interest both enthusiast and amateur — in particular, the beautiful medieval town of St-Émilion. The wines have an easy charm, perhaps assisted by the dominance of Merlot in the blend, and offer a good choice, ranging from the higher profile Crus Classés to the lesser-known but more affordable petits châteaux.

St-Émilion has a complex soil structure and varying topography. Indeed, it is the range of soil types and the general lie of the land, along with the skills of the winemaker, that have a major bearing on the variety of styles and the quality of the wines. The tour sets out to unravel this influencing factor, at the same time highlighting the historical and geographical wealth of the region.

The Tour

From the town of Libourne take the D243 in the direction of St-Émilion, crossing the railway line and passing Ch. Tailhas in the south-west corner of Pomerol AC. Soon after, a signpost declaring '*Vous êtes dans le Vignoble de St-Émilion – Cité Médiévale*' indicates the western boundary of St-Émilion AC. The vineyards are immediately visible in the fairly flat landscape, spanning both sides of the road.

A little further on is the entrance to Ch. Figeac, marked by two small stone pillars carved with the name of the château. The vineyards of Ch. Figeac at one time included those of neighbouring Ch. Cheval-Blanc. These two great estates are the only Premiers Grands Crus Classés to be located beyond the town's reaches, and it is the soil here, known as *graves anciennes,* which is the key to their success. Looking north-east from Figeac's 18th-century château and park, there is a series of undulating knolls running on through Ch. Cheval-Blanc and into Pomerol, just beyond. Similar to the soil found in the best Cru Classé vineyards of the Médoc, these gravel mounds are more suited to Cabernet Sauvignon than are other parts of St-Émilion — hence, Ch. Figeac's almost Médoc-style composition of 70 per cent Cabernet Sauvignon and Cabernet Franc. Long-lived Ch. Cheval-Blanc has an even more unusual blend for these parts: 60 per cent Cabernet Franc and 40 per cent Merlot.

Continue toward the town of St-Émilion with its famous steepled bell-tower, surrounded by a sea of vineyards. Turn right off the D243 past Ch. Laroze, which is run on biodynamic lines, and turn left at the first junction. The landscape is dotted with the buildings of numerous

TOUR SUMMARY

Starting from Libourne, the route encompasses the serene countryside and accessible vineyards of St-Émilion AC. A short walking tour of the beautiful and historically fascinating town of St-Émilion is followed by a visit to the various satellite ACs. The tour ends in St-Émilion.

Distance covered 70km (45 miles).

Time needed 5½ hours.

Terrain The route mainly uses *départementale* roads, which are occasionally winding but easy to follow.

Hotels There is a small selection of good hotels in and around the town of St-Émilion, encompassing a full range of price categories. The options in the surrounding countryside are more limited.

Restaurants St-Émilion offers the greatest choice of places to eat in the area. However, the best and the worst are located here, so choose carefully.

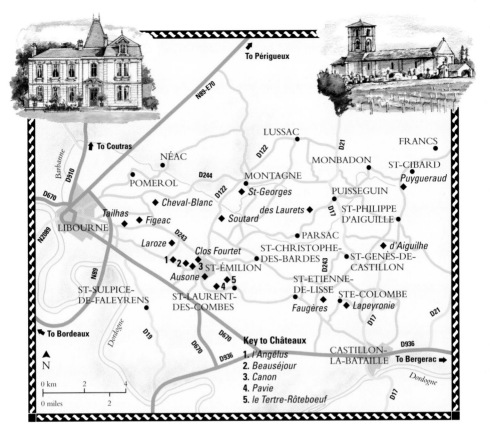

To Périgueux

N89-E70

To Coutras

Barbanne

D910

D670

POMEROL

NÉAC

D244

D112

LUSSAC

MONBADON

D21

FRANCS

ST-CIBARD

Puygueraud

MONTAGNE

St-Georges

PUISSEGUIN

ST-PHILIPPE
D'AIGUILLE

Cheval-Blanc

des Laurets

D21

Tailhas

Soutard

Figeac

D243

LIBOURNE

N2089

Laroze

Clos Fourtet

1 2 3 ST-ÉMILION

Ausone

4 5

PARSAC

ST-CHRISTOPHE-
DES-BARDES

d'Aiguilhe

ST-GENÈS-DE-
CASTILLON

D243

N89

ST-SULPICE-
DE-FALEYRENS

ST-LAURENT-
DES-COMBES

ST-ETIENNE-
DE-LISSE

Faugères

STE-COLOMBE

Lapeyronie

D17

D21

To Bordeaux

Dordogne

D19

D670

D670

D936

Key to Châteaux

1. l'Angélus
2. Beauséjour
3. Canon
4. Pavie
5. le Tertre-Rôteboeuf

CASTILLON-
LA-BATAILLE

To Bergerac

Dordogne

D936

D17

N

0 km   2   4

0 miles   2

*Map illustrations: (above left) Ch.
Laroze; (above right) the church of
St-Martin-de-Mazerat.*

domaines, emphasizing the relatively small size of properties
in the region. The road begins to climb through the limestone and clay slopes of St-Émilion, finally breaking out in
a copse at the revamped cellars of Ch. l'Angélus. This property was newly promoted to Premier Grand Cru Classé in
1996 and has vineyards both on the slopes and on what is
known as the Pied-de-Côtes below. The denser sandy topsoil of the lower vineyards is considered less conducive to
producing great wines, but, with investment, wine-making
skill and attention to detail, the owners have proved that
this terroir can be manipulated to positive effect.

Beyond Ch. l'Angélus the road climbs the slopes, round-
ing a bend past Ch. Beauséjour, a less well-known but
remarkably consistent Premier Grand Cru Classé, to arrive
at the gates of Ch. Canon. The property was named after a
naval officer, Jacques Kanon, and produces fine, structured
wines from grapes grown on the thin, well-drained topsoils
of the limestone plateau. Behind the 18th-century château
and its cellars, which contain a battery of polished wooden
vats, catch a glimpse of the square bell-tower of the 12th-
century church of St-Martin-de-Mazerat before heading for
the ramparts and town of St-Émilion.

The vineyards of Clos Fourtet extend over a plateau
bordering the town, and it is worth visiting the 14ha of

cellars here, formed after limestone rock was extracted to construct the town. The quality of the wines is inconsistent but they are usually ageworthy. There is a labyrinthine network of passageways and cellars under the town and surrounding vineyards, which are used by a number of other châteaux for aging wines.

Head on foot into town past the Collegiate church, leaving the car in sight of the Great Wall, the only remaining ruins of a 13th-century Franciscan Friary. The centrally sited Place des Créneaux has a spectacular view out over the rooftops down to the Dordogne Valley beyond. The astonishing monolithic church is located just below the square. Following the lane that runs past the square King's Tower, the road eventually slips under a tunnel to arrive at Ch. Ausone. The steeply sloping vineyard of this tiny but prestigious Cru has a complex soil structure and an exceptional mesoclimate due to its southerly exposure, which assist in producing firm, elegant, long-lived wines. Amble back through the centre of the town, perhaps stopping off at one of the many cafés and restaurants.

Now head on the D122 toward the village of Montagne – catch a glimpse of Ch. Soutard to the east, with its impressive 18th-century château and sweep of vineyards, one of a number of properties that hug the road. The stone ruins of windmills strewn around the hilltops emphasize the exposed nature of the terrain and the sometimes blustery climate. The road now descends to the Barbanne river, really more of a stream, which marks the boundary between St-Émilion and the satellite ACs of St-Georges and Montagne. On a hill above the tiny river valley, the elegant Ch. St-Georges with its four conical turrets dominates the skyline. The vineyards have a wonderful sloping exposure and the wines of this estate can be every bit as good as a St-Émilion proper.

After visiting Montagne's wine museum, Ecomusée du Libournais, turn eastward to Puisseguin, where a row of cypress trees greets the visitor. The local co-operative, les Producteurs Réunis, is shared by growers from both the Lussac and Montagne satellite ACs – it produces 45 per cent of the wines of Lussac and 35 per cent of Puisseguin and has a range to taste. South-west of the village, the Napoleon III-style Ch. des Laurets has 80ha of vineyard in a single block and is one of the largest properties in the Libournais. Recent investment has helped to improve the quality of the wines, which are firm and well-balanced.

Leaving Puisseguin in the direction of Francs, the road passes the beautiful 14th-century château of Monbadon. At the crossroads head for St-Philippe-d'Aiguille, skirting Bordeaux-Côtes de Francs AC and passing the entrance to Ch. Puygueraud, the top estate in the AC. This is the

Vineyards grow very close to the town of St-Émilion, the Roman town at the centre of Bordeaux's most historic region.

property of George Thienpont, whose family have made the small Côtes de Francs AC their fiefdom, having invested in the region as far back as 1946 and have since added Châteaux Laclaverie and les Charmes-Godard to their list. Continue into Côtes de Castillon AC, passing the military radar installation at St-Philippe d'Aiguille – situated at 119m (390ft), the highest point in the whole of the Gironde region. Follow signs for Ch. d'Aiguilhe, one of the oldest properties in Bordeaux, with 14th-century château ruins. Increased investment and improved wine-making and viticultural techniques have lifted this estate out of the doldrums. Along with a number of other châteaux, it is providing a new momentum for the AC.

The lower gate out of Ch. d'Aiguilhe opens on to a wooded country lane leading almost all the way to St-Genès-de-Castillon. From here, head to Ste-Colombe along an equally meandering road, turning past Ch. Lapeyronie and the village's Romanesque church in the direction of Ch. Faugères. The sloping vineyards of this property straddle the Côtes de Castillon and St-Émilion ACs and a wine from each is produced. One of the results of the cash injection here is the ultra-modern *cuverie*, designed by the team of architects that built the cellars at Ch. Pichon-Longueville in Pauillac. The gleaming stainless steel vats are, unusually, conical in shape, imitating wooden vats.

To complete the tour, take the road back to St-Émilion via the tiny villages of St-Etienne-de-Lisse and St-Laurent des-Combes, passing below the brilliant but unclassified Ch. le Tertre-Rôteboeuf. The flat, sandy plane of the Dordogne valley, the greater part of St-Émilion AC, is visible to the south. To the north-west the vineyards of the slopes reappear, culminating in those of Ch. Pavie with the town of St-Émilion sitting prominently above.

The distinctive architecture of Ch. St-Georges dominates the valley in the St-Émilion satellite AC of St-Georges.

St-Émilion Fact File

The historic town of St-Émilion is the centre of the wine region, with a small but good range of hotels and restaurants providing a lively base for the visitor.

Information

Ecomusée du Libournais
33570 Montagne. Tel 05 57 74 56 89.
Museum of local history and viticulture.

Maison du Vin de Lussac-St-Émilion
33570 Lussac. Tel 05 57 74 50 35.

Maison du Vin de Montagne-St-Émilion
33570 Montagne. Tel 05 57 74 60 13.

Maison du Vin de Puisseguin-St-Émilion
33570 Puisseguin. Tel 05 57 74 50 62.

Maison du Vin de St-Émilion
Place Pierre Meyrat, 33330 St-Émilion. Tel 05 57 55 50 55; fax 05 57 24 65 57.
Information, wines and wine-tasting classes. The *Guide des Vins du St-Émilion* is useful.

Office du Tourisme
Place des Créneaux, 33330 St-Émilion. Tel 05 57 24 72 03; fax 05 57 74 47 15.
A list of wine cellars open to visitors is available.

Syndicat Viticole des Côtes de Castillon
6 Allées de la République, 33350 Castillon-la-Bataille. Tel 05 57 40 00 88; fax 05 57 40 06 31.
The *Guide des Châteaux* is helpful.

Syndicat Viticole de St-Émilion
BP15, rue Guadet, 33330 St-Émilion. Tel 05 57 55 50 50; fax 05 57 24 65 57.

Markets

Castillon-la-Bataille – Monday
St-Émilion – Sunday

Festivals and Events

St-Émilion's many festivals include the *Fête du Printemps* in

The town of St-Émilion has many cafés and restaurants – but some are better value than others.

June and the *Ban des Vendanges* in September – concerts and wine-tastings are held in various châteaux. The Portes Ouvertes weekend in St-Émilion falls in May, while the Côtes de Castillon holds several open days in July and August. The satellites offer a weekend of food and wine-tasting in October.

Where to Buy Wine

Wines are available from all the Maisons du Vin. Many châteaux offer cellar-door sales, and there are a number of wine shops in St-Émilion.
L'Envers du Décor
Rue du Clocher, 33330 St-Émilion.
Welcoming bar serving a selection of regional wines.

Where to Stay and Eat

Hôtel/Restaurant Bonne Auberge Ⓕ
Rue 8 Mai 1945, 33350 Castillon-la-Bataille. Tel 05 57 40 11 56. Ⓕ
Brasserie and restaurant service. Hotel with 10 rooms.

Hôtel Bonsai Relais-Restaurant le Clos Rivallon Ⓗ Ⓡ
Bois de l'Or, Route de Castillon, 33330 St-Émilion. Tel 05 57 25 25 07; fax 05 57 25 26 59. Ⓕ Ⓕ

Modern family hotel beyond the town walls. Restaurant offers regional cuisine.

Hôtel/Restaurant Château Grand Barrail Ⓗ Ⓡ
Route de Libourne, 33330 St-Émilion. Tel 05 57 55 37 00; fax 05 57 55 37 49. Ⓕ Ⓕ Ⓕ
Luxury international hotel with spacious rooms just outside the town. The cuisine is now of a high standard.

Restaurant le Clos du Roy Ⓡ
Rue de la Petite Fontaine, 33330 St-Émilion. Tel 05 57 74 41 55; fax 05 57 74 45 13. Ⓕ Ⓕ
Refined, inventive cuisine.

Auberge de la Commanderie Ⓗ
Rue des Cordeliers, 33330 St-Émilion. Tel 05 57 24 70 19; fax 05 57 74 44 53. Ⓕ
Comfortable hotel with 18 rooms.

Restaurant Francis Goullée Ⓡ
Rue Guadet, 33330 St-Émilion. Tel 05 57 24 70 49; fax 05 57 74 47 96. Ⓕ Ⓕ
Excellent regional cuisine. Try the *Menu Dégustation des Produits de Terroir.*

Hôtel le Logis des Remparts Ⓗ
Rue Guadet, 33330 St-Émilion. Tel 05 57 24 70 43; fax 05 57 74 47 44. Ⓕ Ⓕ
Tidy, efficient, family-run hotel. Terrace overlooking the old town walls.

Hostellerie de Plaisance Ⓗ Ⓡ
Place du Clocher, 33330 St-Émilion. Tel 05 57 24 72 32; fax 05 57 74 41 11. Ⓕ Ⓕ Ⓕ
Classic establishment with well-executed dishes and wonderful views over the town. There are 10 rooms available.

Restaurant le Tertre Ⓡ
Rue du Tertre-de-la-Tente, 33330 St-Émilion. Tel 05 57 74 46 33; fax 05 57 74 49 87. Ⓕ
Well-prepared regional dishes at reasonable prices.

Wines and Wine Villages

The region of St-Émilion has enormous charm. The historic town itself is a delight, the surrounding villages attractive and the châteaux welcoming to visitors.

Bordeaux-Côtes de Francs AC
Small AC with only 400ha of vineyards. The red wines can be aged and there is a small production of white wines – both are good value.
Best producers: de Francs, la Claverie, les Charmes-Godard, Moulin-la-Pitié, la Prade, Puyanché, Puygueraud.

Côtes de Castillon AC
The red wines of this AC have improved greatly in recent years and now represent one of the best buys in Bordeaux.
Best producers: d'Aiguilhe, de Belcier, Blanzac, Cantegrive, la Clairière-Laithwaite, Côte-Monpezat, Cap-de-Faugères, Lapeyronie, Peyrou, Poupille, Robin, Vieux-Ch.-Champs-de-Mars.

Crus Classés
The St-Émilion classification dates from 1955 and is reviewed every 10 years or so, most recently in 1996. The châteaux, which must qualify for Grand Cru AC, submit a demand for classification which is decided on by an independent committee. There are 2 levels: Grand Cru Classé (of which there are presently 55) and Premier Grand Cru Classé, the élite class, with a list of 13 châteaux. The latter are further divided into 2 divisions: A and B, with only 2 properties in the former.
Premiers Grands Crus Classés:
(A) Ausone, Cheval-Blanc; (B) l'Angélus, Beau-Séjour-Bécot, Beauséjour, Belair, Canon, Clos Fourtet, la Gaffelière, Magdelaine, Pavie, Trottevieille.
Grands Crus Classés: l'Arrosée, Balestard-la-Tonnelle, Bellevue, Bergat, Berliquet, Cadet-Bon, Cadet-Piola, Canon-la-Gaffelière, Cap-de-Mourlin, Chauvin, Clos des Jacobins, Clos de l'Oratoire, Clos St-Martin, la Clotte, la Clusière, Corbin, Corbin-Michotte, la Couspaude, Couvent des Jacobins, Curé-Bon, Dassault, la Dominique, Faurie de Souchard,
Fonplégade, Fonroque, Franc-Mayne, Grand-Mayne, Grand-Pontet, Grandes-Murailles, Gaudet-St-Julien, Haut-Corbin, Haut-Sarpe, Lamarzelle, Laniote, Larcis-Ducasse, Larmande, Laroque, Laroze, Matras, Moulin-du-Cadet, Pavie-Decesse, Pavie-Macquin, Petit-Faurie-de-Soutard, le Prieuré, Ripeau, St-Georges-Côte-Pavie, la Serre, Soutard, Tertre-Daugay, la Tour-du-Pin-Figeac (Giraud-Bélivier), la Tour-du-Pin-Figeac (Moueix), la Tour-Figeac, Troplong-Mondot, Villemaurine, Yon-Figeac.

The ancient streets of St-Émilion are fascinating to wander through – as are the cellars beneath.

Lussac-St-Émilion AC
The most northerly of the St-Émilion satellite ACs. The climate is cooler and the soils varied, as are the wines. Just outside the village of Lussac is a gallic megalith at the Tertre de Picampeau.
Best producers: Barbe-Blanche, Bel-Air, la Grenière, Lyonnat, LES PRODUCTEURS RÉUNIS.

Montagne-St-Émilion AC
The largest of the St-Émilion satellite ACs, absorbing the wines of Parsac-St-Émilion in 1982. The south-facing sites and soils provide the potential for full-bodied wines. The village of Montagne has a museum and an interesting Romanesque church.

Best producers: Bonneau, Calon, Corbin, Faizeau, des Laurets, Montaiguillon, Négrit, Roc-de-Calon, Roudier, Vieux-Ch.-St-André.

Puisseguin-St-Émilion AC
The wines from this satellite AC are usually firm and muscular. The village of Puisseguin boasts a Romanesque church and a millstone-cutter's cave, Taillerie de Meules. Just outside are the ruins of the 14th-century fortress, Château Malengin.
Best producers: l'Anglais, Durand-Laplagne, Guibot-la-Fourvieille, des Laurets, LES PRODUCTEURS RÉUNIS, Soleil.

St-Émilion AC
The basic AC of St-Émilion, covering just over 5000ha, an area which corresponds to the 8 communes that fell within the medieval jurisdiction of St-Émilion. The town has a host of architectural monuments including 9th-century catacombs, an 11th-century monolithic church, the Great Wall and the 13th-century King's Tower.
Best producers: Union des Producteurs de St-Émilion.

St-Émilion Grand Cru AC
Superior AC to St-Émilion AC, covering the same area but demanding lower yields, higher minimum levels of alcohol and a further tasting analysis.
Best producers: L'ANGÉLUS, AUSONE, Beau-Séjour-Bécot, Beauséjour, Belair, Bellefont-Belcier, CANON, CHEVAL-BLANC, CLOS FOURTET, Carteau-Côtes-Daugay, Destieux, Faugères, FIGEAC, Fleur-Cardinale, Fombrauge, Gueyrosse, Haut-Segottes, Haut-Villet, Magdelaine, Monbousquet, Moulin-St-Georges, PAVIE, le Tertre-Rôteboeuf, Valandraud.

St-Georges-St-Émilion AC
The smallest of the satellite ACs, with only 180ha. Producers can declare their wines under either Montagne AC or St-Georges AC.
Best producers: Calon, Vieux-Montaiguillon, St-André-Corbin, ST-GEORGES, Tour-du-Pas-St-Georges.

The 8ha vineyard of Ch. le Gay is situated on the northern edge of the Pomerol plateau in the vicinity of Ch. Pétrus. The soils are typically clay based, with gravel outcrops to the north of the upper terrace. As with most estates in Pomerol, this is a modest-looking, family-owned property. The wines are marketed and distributed by the Libourne négociant J-P Moueix. The vineyard is old and well protected from the wind. The vines are extremely low yielding. The wines, made from equal proportions of Merlot and Cabernet Franc, are, consequently, powerful rich and dense, needing a number of years' bottle age to mellow out the rather tough tannic structure.

Vieux-Château-Certan produces wines with a high proportion of Cabernets Sauvignon and Franc in the blend, making them seem more like Médocs than Pomerols.

Pomerol and Fronsac

It has to be said that, at first glance, Pomerol has little to excite the visitor – an almost monotonous stretch of vineyards and a scattering of modest-looking estates is all that meets the eye. But this small AC of only 785ha produces some of the finest and most expensive wines in the world. The key to Pomerol's great estates, the medley of flavours in its wines and the opulence derived from Merlot, Pomerol's essential grape variety, lies in something much less discernible – the geological intricacies of the soil.

Across the Isle river in Fronsac the scenario changes. The landscape here is one of hill slopes and plateaux, and the region is less well known, despite a reputation, held from as far back as the 18th century, for turning out long-lived wines of depth and character. To the west, the hilly terrain of Bourg and the more dispersed region of Blaye share a viticultural history dating back to Roman times, and are now producing attractive wines at affordable prices.

The Tour

From Libourne follow the directions for Pomerol via Catusseau. On the outskirts of the town, the first impression is one of neat rows of vines planted on completely flat terrain, but, looking into the distance toward the church spire of Pomerol, a gentle rise in the land is perceptible. The slope, in fact, rises to a plateau, the central core of Pomerol on which all the major estates are situated. Here the soils are a mixture of clay and gravel, the same *graves anciennes* found a little further east at Châteaux Figeac and Cheval-Blanc in St-Émilion. The clay dictates that Merlot is the dominant grape variety, but the nuance from one château to the next changes in accordance with the clay-gravel mix and the blend of grape varieties.

Passing through Catusseau, initially taking the road to Montagne, the estates now begin to appear, each a relatively small entity. The road first winds past the 18th-century château of Beauregard, under new management since 1991 and now producing ripe, plummy Pomerols, and the vineyards of Ch. Petit-Village. Just before reaching the low cellar buildings of Châteaux la Conseillante and l'Évangile, turn left toward Vieux-Château-Certan, whose twin-towered château stands at the crossroads of country lanes. Sixty per cent of the vineyard here is located on *graves anciennes* soils and, accordingly, a higher percentage than is usual of Cabernet Sauvignon and Cabernet Franc is used in the blend (45 per cent), resulting in a wine that has

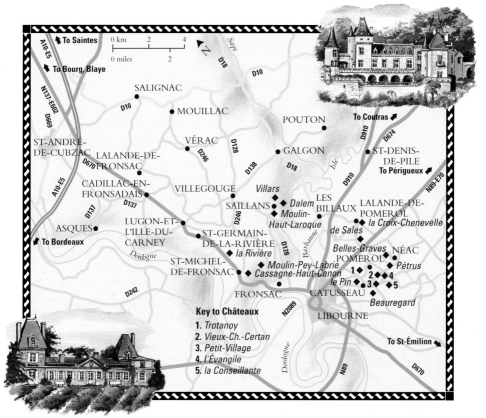

Key to Châteaux
1. *Trotanoy*
2. *Vieux-Ch.-Certan*
3. *Petit-Village*
4. *l'Évangile*
5. *la Conseillante*

Map illustrations: (above) Ch. la Rivière; (below) Vieux-Château-Certan.

something of a Médoc character. Also under the same ownership is the tiny 2ha estate of Ch. le Pin, whose luxurious Merlot-dominated wines fetch huge prices at auction.

Turning toward Néac the road arrives abruptly at the unobtrusive stone cellars of Ch. Pétrus. There is no fine château or striking landmark to indicate the presence of one of the world's most famous wine estates. Instead its assets lie below ground, for here, on the highest part of the Pomerol plateau, the soils are 90 per cent clay mixed with gravel and a broken crust of iron pan. The compact blue clay limits vigour in the vine, regulates water supply and dictates that almost 100 per cent Merlot is used. The resulting wines have an unctuous richness of fruit, exotic aromas and a firm but fine structure.

From Pétrus, take the road through Pomerol – no more than a cluster of houses with the church of St-Jean-de-Pomerol in the centre. Passing Ch. Trotanoy, tucked away in a small copse on the western rim of the plateau, the road dips toward the tree-lined N89. As the road descends, the gravel soils become sandier, producing aromatic wines but without the seductive richness of a full-blown Pomerol. Down on the flat river plain, cross the N89 and follow the signs to Ch. de Sales. With 47.5ha of vines, this is the largest property in the AC and produces soft, generous wines with medium intensity that are typical of this sandier terrain.

Just behind Ch. de Sales, the diminutive Barbanne river marks the division between Pomerol and Lalande-de-Pomerol, but there is little to distinguish the two ACs: the land remains flat, the vineyards broken only by forests and small stone houses. Backtracking a little from Ch. de Sales, the road meanders to the village of Lalande-de-Pomerol. Next to the 12th-century church in the centre of the village, Ch. la Croix-Chenevelle produces velvety wines from a high percentage of Merlot grown on the sandy *graves* soils.

Leaving the village of Lalande-de-Pomerol, cross back over the busy N89 in the direction of Néac, the other commune that comprises the Lalande-de-Pomerol AC. The land rises once more and the countryside becomes a little less monotonous. Just before Néac a little avenue leads to Ch. Belles-Graves. The property sits facing the gentle northern slope of Pomerol on the other side of the Barbanne river, and has vineyards situated on both slope and plateau. The soils have a higher percentage of clay here and the wines are richer, often on a par with a number of their more elevated cousins across the way.

Take the country lane that dips over the Barbanne and head back through Pomerol toward Libourne. Skirting the northern reaches of the town, cross the Isle river in the direction of Fronsac. The restaurant Bord d'Eau on the banks of the Dordogne could provide a welcome stop, or else press on to the village of Fronsac. The region is known as the *pays des tertres,* or land of hillocks, a fact that is immediately proved by the Tertre de Fronsac on the outskirts.

Vineyards in the heart of Canon-Fronsac AC have the right climate and soil for producing firm wines for long aging.

Following the signs for Villegouge and Moulin-Pey-Labrie the road climbs to a butte overlooking the Dordogne and surrounding countryside. The view is exhilarating: a ripple of slopes made up of sedimentary rock known as *molasse de Fronsadais* and small limestone *tertres* dominate the scene; the south-facing slope at Canon drops down to the plain with the meandering Dordogne in the distance; and, on the horizon, the twin towers of the Pont d'Aquitaine at Bordeaux are faintly visible. This is the central core of Fronsac, Canon-Fronsac AC, where sun and soil provide the potential to produce sturdy, long-lived wines. Châteaux Moulin-Pey-Labrie and Cassagne-Haut-Canon, as well as the stable of Moueix properties including Canon and Canon-de-Brem, are some of the estates that are successfully harnessing this potential, as well as adding a touch of finesse through the use of modern vinification techniques and new barrels for aging.

For a more in-depth view of Fronsac, head toward Saillans, where there are a number of excellent producers, such as Châteaux Moulin-Haut-Laroque, Dalem and Villars. If travelling on to Bourg and Blaye, follow the spiralling lane down to St-Michel-de-Fronsac and continue to

St-André-de-Cubzac, passing the striking turreted Ch. la Rivière perched on a slope in a tiny wooded valley. The limestone bedrock of the region, similar to that of St-Émilion, can be seen in the 17th-century cellars created underground from limestone quarries.

The Côtes de Bourg starts just north-west of St-André-de-Cubzac (see regional map page 5), the vineyards generally close to the Dordogne and Gironde rivers. Follow the road to Bourg, passing a number of châteaux built from locally quarried limestone. Just before Bourg head inland to Tauriac for a better view of the hilly, undulating terrain. Here the vineyard of Ch. Brulesécaille is classically situated on a limestone-clay hump. Further inland in the same commune, Ch. Haut-Macô is more of an anomaly, with a mix of soils and a high percentage of Cabernet Sauvignon. On the other side of the sleepy town of Bourg, the Baroque Ch. Tayac overlooks the Gironde. The warm mesoclimate produced by the estuary is shown by the number of palm trees.

The Côtes de Blaye is far more dispersed and therefore more difficult to visit. Ch. Loumède provides a good example of what careful, selective wine-making can achieve on clay-limestone hill sites around the town of Blaye itself. From Blaye, a ferry crosses over to the Médoc, or take the inland road back east toward Bordeaux, travelling through a mix of vineyards, forest, pasture and arable land, making the detour via Cubnezais to visit Ch. Bertinerie. A total restructuring of this domaine, including modern trellising in the vineyards and investment in new barrels, has shown what can be achieved in this varied AC.

In the Côtes de Bourg, vineyards are never situated very far from the Dordogne river, which provides a warm mesoclimate.

Pomerol and Fronsac Fact File

Pomerol is less accessible to visitors than other regions in Bordeaux, but Lalande-de-Pomerol is making efforts to attract visitors. Useful touring guides with names, addresses and telephone numbers of producers are available from the Maisons du Vin in Fronsac, Bourg and Blaye.

Information

Maison du Vin des Côtes du Bourg
Place de l'Eperon, 33710 Bourg. Tel 05 57 94 80 20; fax 05 57 94 80 21.
Information and wines for purchase.

Maison du Vin de Fronsac
33126 Fronsac. Tel 05 57 51 80 51. Tel 05 57 25 98 19.
Information and wines for purchase.

Maison du Vin des Premières Côtes de Blaye
11 cours Vauban, 33390 Blaye. Tel 05 57 42 91 19; fax 05 57 42 85 28.
Information and wines for purchase.

Syndicat Viticole et Agricole de Lalande-de-Pomerol
33500 Lalande-de-Pomerol. Tel 05 57 25 21 60.

Syndicat Viticole et Agricole de Pomerol
33500 Pomerol. Tel 05 57 25 06 88; fax 05 57 25 06 88.

Markets
Blaye – Wednesday and Saturday
Bourg – Sunday
Libourne – Sunday

Festivals and Events
The wine organization Confrérie les Hospitaliers de Pomerol hold the *Fête de la Fleur* to celebrate flowering in the vineyards on the first Sunday in June. The Confrérie des Baillis de Lalande-de-Pomerol organizes a festival around a changing theme, also in June. The Confrérie des Gentilhommes du Duché de Fronsac celebrates the *Fête de la Gerbande* at the end of the harvest in October. A number of ACs have started to organize Portes Ouvertes weekends:

Many of the top châteaux in Pomerol can be difficult to visit – head for the less well-known names.

Bourg in May, Lalande-de-Pomerol in June and Fronsac in October. On the last weekend in January there is a Marché au Vin de Blaye held in the old citadel in Blaye.

Where to Buy Wine
The Maisons du Vin in Bourg, Blaye and Fronsac all have wines available for purchase at cellar door prices. Châteaux in these ACs and in Lalande-de-Pomerol are usually happy to sell direct to the public. Excepting one or two domaines, there is little direct selling in Pomerol.

Where to Stay and Eat
Hotels and restaurants are rather sparse. For a better selection look to St-Émilion.
Restaurant au Sarment (R)
33240 St-Gervais. Tel 05 57 43 44 73; fax 05 57 43 90 28. (F)(F)
Characterful stone building in this village in the Côtes de Bourg. Hearty regional cuisine.

Restaurant Bord d'Eau (R)
'Poinsonnet' – route de Libourne, 33126 Fronsac. Tel 05 57 51 99 91; fax 05 57 25 11 56. (F)(F)

The best place in the region to sample a selection of wines from Fronsac AC. Classic cuisine is served on the banks of the Dordogne river.

Le Bistro Chanzy (R)
16 rue Chanzy, 33500 Libourne. Tel 05 57 51 84 26. (F)
Situated conveniently near the railway station, this pleasant place serves the usual bistro fare and also offers a good selection of wines.

Restaurant Chez Servais (R)
N89, 33570 les Artigues de Lussac. Tel 05 57 24 31 95. (F)(F)
Located just off the main road at the local aerodrome. Boasts slightly more inventive cuisine than the norm, based on regional produce.

Hôtel/Restaurant la Citadelle (H)(R)
Place d'Armes, 33390 Blaye. Tel 05 57 42 17 10; fax 05 57 42 10 34. (F)(F)
Impressive location in the citadel with a view out over the Gironde river. Standard restaurant and 21 rooms.

Clos St-Michel (H)
33126 St-Michel-de-Fronsac. Tel 05 57 24 95 81. (F)
Good value bed and breakfast accommodation in the heart of Canon-Fronsac AC.

Hôtel /Restaurant la Closerie des Vignes (H)(R)
Village des Arnauds, 33710 St-Ciers-de-Canesse. Tel 05 57 64 81 90; fax 05 57 64 94 44. (F)(F)
A 'Relais de Silence' in the middle of the Bourg vineyards. There are 9 modern rooms, regional cuisine and a small, well-selected list of local wines.

Restaurant la Filadière (R)
Lieu-dit 'Furt', 33710 Gauriac. Tel 05 57 64 94 05; fax 05 57 64 94 06. (F)
On the banks of the Gironde river, this establishment serves a lighter cuisine of fish, cold dishes and salads.

Wines and Wine Villages

The tiny but renowned estates, some consisting merely of one vineyard, are the major draw in Pomerol. There is little to see in Lalande-de-Pomerol, but the wines are of interest in terms of character and price. The countryside in Fronsac is delightful and the wines now represent some of the best buys in Bordeaux. The Côtes de Bourg and Blaye have a more ancient history, greater architectural interest and the draw of the Gironde. The hilly landscape in Bourg is attractive, while the town of Blaye has a certain allure.

Canon-Fronsac AC   AC in the heart of the Fronsac region consisting of some 300ha. The generally south-facing slopes and limestone-marl soils produce full, firm wines that benefit from bottle age.
Best producers: Barrabaque, CANON, Canon-de-Brem, Canon-Moueix, CASSAGNE-HAUT-CANON, Grand-Renouil, la Fleur-Cailleau, MOULIN-PEY-LABRIE.

Côtes de Blaye AC   The AC generally used for white wines produced in the Blaye region. Sémillon, Sauvignon, Muscadelle and Colombard are the permitted grape varieties.

Standing on the right bank of the Gironde, the town of Blaye has a harbour that is still in use, a bustling market and impressive citadel. This 17th-century fortress and town was built by Vauban, and still has an active community in its midst.
Best producers: Haut-Grelot, Cave des Hauts de Gironde (Marcillac).

Côtes de Bourg AC
Essentially red wine AC covering some 3600ha on the right bank of the Gironde. The region benefits from the warming influence of the Gironde and Dordogne rivers and a number of well-exposed limestone-clay hillslopes. Merlot is the principal grape variety.

Just south of Blaye the sleepy town of Bourg stands almost at the confluence of the Dordogne and the Gironde. A place of steep, winding lanes, it has a modest citadel of interest. The harbour, formerly used for the salt trade, is now plied by pleasure boats.

Best producers: BRULESÉCAILLE, Bujan, Falfas, Fougas, Gravettes-Samonac, Guerry, HAUT-MACÒ, Macay, Mercier, Nodoz, Roc-de-Cambes, Rousset, TAYAC.

Fronsac AC   Right bank AC just to the west of Libourne making much improved wines from a blend of Merlot, Cabernet Franc and Cabernet Sauvignon. The 800ha of

Strategically located on the Dordogne river, Libourne has always been an important centre for merchants.

vineyards surround Canon-Fronsac AC.

The village of Fronsac houses the Maison du Vin de Fronsac, and there is also a Romanesque church which is worth a visit.
Best producers: de Carles, Dalem, la Dauphine, Fontenil, la Grave, Haut-Lariveau, Moulin-Haut-Laroque, LA RIVIÈRE, la Rousselle, la Vieille-Cure, Villars.

Lalande-de-Pomerol AC
Satellite AC just to the north of Pomerol, making Merlot-dominated wines with a rich fruit character but without the

intensity of its more august neighbour.

The small village of Lalande-de-Pomerol, from which the AC takes its name, is of little interest apart from its 12th-century church.
Best producers: Annereaux, BELLES-GRAVES, Bertineau-St-Vincent, Clos de l'Église, LA CROIX-CHENEVELLE, la Croix-St-André, Fougeailles, Garraud, Grand-Ormeau, Haut-Chaigneau, Haut-Surget, Sergant, Siaurac, de Viaud.

Libourne   Principal town of the Libournais region, situated at the confluence of the Dordogne and Isle rivers. It also serves as the headquarters for the right bank négociants.

Néac   Quiet village and commune that is part of the Lalande-de-Pomerol AC. Wines from this commune can be labelled Néac AC, but in reality this rarely happens.

Pomerol AC   Small but prestigious AC making some of the most expensive wines in Bordeaux – and, indeed, the world. Merlot grown on the clay-gravel soils that are prevalent in these parts produces rich, opulent wines with almost exotic flavours.
Best producers: Beauregard, Bon-Pasteur, la Cabanne, Certan-de-May, Clinet, LA CONSEILLANTE, la Croix-de-Gay, Domaine de l'Église, l'Église-Clinet, l'Évangile, la Fleur-Pétrus, le Gay, Gazin, Gombaude-Guillot, la Grave-à-Pomerol, Lafleur, Latour-à-Pomerol, Petit-Village, PÉTRUS, le Pin, DE SALES, Trotanoy, VIEUX-CHÂTEAU-CERTAN.

Premières Côtes de Blaye AC
Dispersed AC on the right bank of the Gironde for red wines and a minuscule amount of white. Merlot is usually the dominant variety for the reds.
Best producers: BERTINERIE, Cave des Hauts-de-Gironde (Marcillac), Haut-Grelot, les Graves, les Jonqueyres, LOUMÈDE, Monconseil-Gazin, Roland la Garde, Philippe Raguenot.

A-Z of Main Wine Producers

Bordeaux's reputation is built around the château, or wine estate. The Médoc, more than anywhere, perpetuates the ideal of a grand house, extensive landholdings and palatial cellars, but the majority of châteaux in Bordeaux are more modest family affairs. Château wines are made and bottled on the property itself.

Co-operatives play an important role in absorbing the production of thousands of vinegrowers, each with small parcels of land, by selling them under co-operative labels, or by calling them 'château bottled' wines if they are produced from a precise vineyard. The négociants, or merchants, who may or may not be château owners themselves, act as brokers, buying and selling the wines from individual châteaux. Some market their own brands made from grapes, juice or wines bought from the winegrowers or co-operatives. The following is a selection of the leading producers in the region.

Key to Symbols

Visiting arrangements ⊘ Visitors welcome ⊘ By appointment ⊗ No visitors.
Wine styles made ⑨ Red wine ⑨ White wine ⑨ Rosé wine. Page numbers refer to the tour featuring the producer.

Château d'Aiguilhe
St-Philippe d'Aiguille, 33350 Castillon-la-Bataille. Tel 05 57 40 60 10; fax 05 57 40 63 56. ⊘ ⑨ pp.59, 61
One of the oldest properties in the Bordeaux region, this has been owned by Spanish Cava producers Raventós i Blanc since 1989. It is one of a number of much-improved estates in Côtes de Castillon AC, and produces rich, ripe Merlot-based wines with an elegant structure.

Château l'Angélus
33330 St-Émilion. Tel 05 57 24 71 39; fax 05 57 24 68 56. ⊘ ⑨ pp.57, 61
This estate was recently promoted to Premier Grand Cru Classé and is one of the stars of St-Émilion AC, with a new *cuverie*, barrel cellars and reception room. The vineyard is less favourably sited in the *pied de côtes* but this has been counterbalanced by skilful wine-making and investment in modern technology. The wines are rich, full and polished. Second wine: le Carillon de Angélus.

Château Ausone
33330 St-Émilion. Tel 05 57 24 68 88; fax 05 57 74 47 39. ⊗ ⑨ pp.58, 61
Only 27,000 bottles of wine a year are produced at this tiny but prestigious estate, named after the 4th-century Roman poet Ausonius. The 7ha vineyard, situated on the steep southern slopes of St-Émilion, can be seen on the edge of the town. The wines are aged in naturally cool limestone cellars and are long-lived and firmly structured, but with an elegance and poise that are sometimes astonishing.

Château Belles-Graves
33500 Néac. Tel 05 57 51 09 61; fax 05 57 51 01 41. ⊘ ⑨ pp.66, 69
Separated from Pomerol by the tiny Barbanne river, this estate in Lalande-de-Pomerol AC has the potential to produce the type of ripe, flavoursome wines associated with its more august neighbour. The vineyard is located on the clay-gravel hillslope overlooking the Barbanne and is planted predominantly with Merlot.

Château Bertinerie
33620 Cubnezais. Tel 05 57 68 70 74; fax 05 57 68 01 03. ⊘ ⑨ ⑨ pp.67, 69
This estate is one of Bordeaux's more revolutionary domaines and an inspiration for others in Premières Côtes de Blaye AC. The vineyard has been refitted to the 'lyre' system of trellising to obtain greater ripeness of fruit, and the cellars have been totally modernized. The top-of-the-range wines are labelled Château Haut-Bertinerie. The red is concentrated and softly tannic and the white is 100 per cent Sauvignon, barrel-fermented, full, round and aromatic. The wines of the estate's second label, Château Bertinerie, are crisp, fresh and fruity.

Château Beychevelle
33250 St-Julien-Beychevelle. Tel 05 56 73 20 70; fax 05 56 73 20 71. ⊘ ⑨ pp.15, 21, 27
Travelling north from Bordeaux, imposing Beychevelle is the first estate reached in St-Julien AC. The name derives from the lowering of the sail, or *baisse-voile* salute, that passing ships used to give to a former owner, who was also an Admiral of the French fleet. The wines of this Quatrième Cru are usually soft, generous and surprisingly drinkable when young, but they can also be aged for 15–20 years. Second wine: Réserve de l'Amiral.

Château Biston-Brillette
33480 Moulis-en-Médoc. Tel 05 56 58 22 86; fax 05 56 58 13 16. ⊘ ⑨ pp.27, 29
The estate was created from virtually nothing in 1963 and has now risen to 22ha. The wines have crisp, bright fruit and are well structured. This is one of the value-for-money estates in

Moulis AC, run as a family affair by brothers Serge and Jean-Paul Barbarin.

Château Bonnet
33420 Grézillac. Tel 05 57 25 58 58; fax 05 57 74 98 59. ⊘⊙⊙ pp.51, 53
Situated in the north of the Entre-Deux-Mers, Ch. Bonnet is the vast viticultural domaine owned by the irrepressible André Lurton. The selection of wines includes a crisp, fruity Entre-Deux-Mers, a barrel-fermented version of the same and two red Cuvées, one barrel-aged. Considering the volume produced, the quality is remarkably consistent. The 18th-century château with landscaped gardens is a private residence.

Château Brulesécaille
33710 Tauriac. Tel 05 57 68 40 31; fax 05 57 68 21 27. ⊘⊙ pp.67, 69
Mentioned in the 1868 edition of Cocks et Féret as a 'cru Bourgeois' of the Côtes de Bourg, Ch. Brulesécaille continues to produce well-crafted wines today. The name refers to the burning of the vine cuttings following pruning. The vineyard is located on a clay-limestone hillock and has a wonderful view of the Dordogne valley. The wines, which are made from Merlot

and Cabernet and aged in a small percentage of new oak, are excellent value.

Château Canon
33330 St-Émilion. Tel 05 57 24 70 79; fax 05 57 24 68 00. ⊘⊙ pp.57, 61
This estate has been one of the most consistent of St-Émilion's Premiers Grands Crus Classés for a number of years. It will therefore be interesting to see what improvements are made by its new (November 1996) owners, Chanel, the perfume and fashion group. The vineyard is situated predominantly on the limestone plateau just outside the town of St-Émilion. The wines, which are fermented in immaculate oak vats, are concentrated, powerful and structured for long aging. Second wine: Clos J. Kanon.

Château Carsin
33410 Rions. Tel 05 56 76 93 06. Tel 05 56 62 64 80. ⊘⊙⊙ pp.50, 53
A modern domaine in the Premières Côtes de Bordeaux that is of most interest to visitors with some knowledge of the technical aspects of wine-making. The installations are based on those perfected at the Petaluma estate in Adelaide Hills, South Australia. Ch. Carsin's Australian winemaker Mandy Jones applies New World methods for the white wines, while remaining more traditional in her techniques for the reds. There are usually a number of different experiments being conducted at any one time. The whites are rich, round and aromatic with a hint of oak; the reds are fresh and supple.

Château Cassagne-Haut-Canon
33126 St-Michel de Fronsac. Tel 05 57 51 63 98; fax 05 57 51 62 20. ⊘⊙ pp.66, 69
One of the domaines responsible for generating renewed interest in Fronsac and Canon-Fronsac ACs. The vineyard is situated on a small *tertre*, or hill, with a splendid view of the surrounding region. The wines are rich, ripe and concentrated, requiring a certain maturity in the bottle. The special Cuvée la Truffière has a higher percentage of Cabernet Sauvignon, adding elegance and length on the palate. Owner and winemaker Jean-Jacques Dubois provides an enthusiastic exposé of his wines and the AC.

Cellier de la Bastide
33540 Sauveterre-de-Guyenne. Tel 05 56 61 55 21; fax 05 56 71 60 11. ⊘⊙⊙⊙ pp.50, 53
This co-operative in the Entre-Deux-Mers was created in 1934. Until 1973 only white wines were produced but reds now represent two-thirds of the volume. The Cellier, however, is still noted for its white wines, with Sauvignon gradually gaining importance in each blend. The Cellier de la Bastide label is usually good value and there are a number of respectable 'château bottled' wines. The shop is open daily for tastings and sales.

Château de Chantegrive
33720 Podensac. Tel 05 56 27 17 38; fax 05 56 27 29 42. ⊘⊙⊙ pp.35, 37
This modern Graves estate was created from virtually nothing in 1967 by owners Françoise and

---

VISITING WINE PRODUCERS

Telephone in advance to ensure that your visit is convenient and that there will be someone there to receive you.
English-speaking guides conduct visits to many of the Cru Classé châteaux. At the smaller estates the owner or winemaker is more likely to show you around; he/she will be more knowledgeable about the domaine, but possibly less fluent in English.

Lunchtime in rural France is still an important occasion, so ensure that you don't arrive at a property between 12 and 2pm.
Holidays are often taken in August and consequently the châteaux may be closed for visits.
Harvest time (early September/mid-October) is a busy time of the year and people may not always have time to stop to help you. Visits are not recommended unless the château employs a full-time guide.
Tastings will probably consist of

samples of the most recently bottled vintage(s). These will be available for purchase at the smaller domaines but not necessarily at the great estates. Do not expect a range of older vintages.
Spittoons are usually provided at tastings, and whether or not you are driving, it is best to make use of them in order to keep a clean palate.
Credit cards are not always accepted as payment for wine purchases, particularly at the smaller properties.

Henri Lévêque. The regular white Graves is crisp and racy, the pricier Cuvée Caroline a richer, more aromatic, barrel-fermented version. The red is supple and fruity. There is also a small amount of sweet Cérons.

Château Cheval-Blanc

33330 St-Émilion. Tel 05 57 55 55 55; fax 05 57 55 55 50. ⊘ ⊕
pp.56, 61
Owned by the Fourcaud-Laussac family since 1832, this is one of Bordeaux's great estates and, with Ch. Ausone, the only other property in St-Émilion to be classified Premier Grand Cru Classé (A). The wines are made from an unusually high percentage of old vine Cabernet Franc (60 per cent) blended with Merlot. This provides elegance, complexity and ageability in the wines. The vineyard soils are composed of a mix of *graves anciennes*, clay and sand. There is an interesting sample cross-section of the soil structure at the château that can be viewed. Second wine: le Petit Cheval.

Domaine de Chevalier

33850 Léognan. Tel 05 56 64 16 16; fax 05 56 64 18 18. ⊘ ⊕ ⊕
pp.34, 37
Property run with great enthusiasm by owner Olivier Bernard and his team. There has been greater ripeness and concentration in recent vintages of the red wines, and the whites, barrel-fermented and made from a majority of Sauvignon Blanc, continue to be steely, aromatic and extremely long-lived. Second wine: l'Esprit de Chevalier.

Château Clarke

33480 Listrac-Médoc. Tel 05 56 58 38 00; fax 05 56 58 26 46. ⊘ ⊕ ⊕ pp.27, 29
Baron Edmond de Rothschild bought this estate in Listrac in 1973 and has invested heavily in

its renovation. Merlot is the dominant grape variety, making a full, ripe wine with firm tannic structure. There is also a white wine, le Merle Blanc.

Château Climens

33720 Barsac. Tel 05 56 27 15 33; fax 05 56 27 21 04. ⊘ ⊕
pp.43, 45
The leading estate in Barsac, producing rich, botrytized wines of extraordinary elegance and freshness from almost 100 per cent Sémillon grapes. The estate, with its 18th-century manor house, sits on the highest point of the Barsac plateau and the vineyard is planted on limestone bedrock which provides excellent natural drainage. It is now owned by sisters Brigitte and Bérénice Lurton. The wines are fermented and aged in oak barrels. Second wine: Les Cyprès de Climens.

Clos Fourtet

33330 St-Émilion. Tel 05 57 24 70 90; fax 05 57 74 46 52. ⊘ ⊕
pp.57, 61
This Premier Grand Cru Classé has a superb location on the north-eastern edge of the town of St-Émilion. A tour of the property includes the *cuverie* and, of most interest, part of the impressive 14ha of limestone cellars that have been quarried on three levels below ground. Typically the wines are made from a high percentage of Merlot (70 per cent) and have an overt fruit character, medium intensity and fine tannic structure. Previously one of St-Émilion's under-achievers, this Cru has restored confidence with recent vintages .

Château Clos Haut-Peyraguey

33210 Bommes. Tel 05 56 76 61 53; fax 05 56 76 69 65. ⊘ ⊕
pp.42, 45
This Sauternes property, classified Premier Cru in 1855, has the unpretentious air of a small family estate. The wines have progressively improved over the last ten years and now rival some of the better-known Crus. The châteaus is ideally

situated on the plateau at Haut-Bommes, and is open daily for tastings.

Clos Jean

33410 Loupiac. Tel 05 56 62 99 83; fax 05 56 62 93 55. ⊘ ⊕ ⊕
pp.43, 45
The vineyard is situated on the slopes of Haut-Loupiac with a splendid view over the Garonne. In the 19th century, Clos Jean's sweet wines were considered on a par with certain Sauternes. Today the better vintages are indeed lush and rich and are excellent value for money.

Château la Conseillante

33500 Pomerol. Tel 05 57 51 12 12; fax 05 57 51 42 42. ⊘ ⊕
pp.64, 69
This property produces the typically rich, succulent, heady wines that characterize the best of Pomerol AC. This family-owned estate still has the feel of a small farm. It has a superb site on Pomerol's high plateau, just opposite Ch. Cheval-Blanc in neighbouring St-Émilion, and close to some of Pomerol's élite: l'Évangile, Petit-Village and Vieux-Château-Certan. Like all Pomerols of this stature, the wines are scarce and expensive, and extremely long-lived.

Château Cos d'Estournel

33180 St-Estèphe. Tel 05 56 73 15 55; fax 05 56 59 72 59. ⊘ ⊕
pp.18, 21
This is one of Bordeaux's greats, much followed and admired. The château itself is one of the Médoc's great follies: a curious mix of Hindu temple and Chinese pagoda. A small museum now graphically recounts the history of the property. The wines are rich, dark and concentrated, the high percentage of Merlot providing a supple texture to the palate.

Domaine de Courteillac

33350 Ruch. Tel 05 57 40 55 65; fax 05 57 40 58 07. ⓐⓑⓒ pp.50, 53

Stéphane Asseo began the resurrection of this boutique winery in the Entre-Deux-Mers in 1982. Some of the vines are over 50 years old. Careful selection and vinification now produce a dense red wine that belies its Bordeaux Supérieur AC. In addition to a regular dry white, a tiny amount of white Cuvée Antholien is made from primarily Sémillon, fermented and aged in 100 per cent new oak barrels.

Château la Croix-Chenevelle

33500 Lalande-de-Pomerol. Tel 05 57 51 99 93; fax 05 57 74 00 63. ⓐⓑ pp.66, 69

Small, go-ahead, family estate making the best of the gravelly soils found in this sector of Lalande-de-Pomerol AC. The wines are made mainly from Merlot and aged in a percentage of new oak barrels, giving them a certain generosity of style similar to a Pomerol without the concentration. Owner Bernard Levrault is one of the younger generation of producers trying to motivate this rather discrete AC.

Château Faugères

St-Etienne-de-Lisse, 33330 St-Émilion. Tel 05 57 40 34 99; fax 05 57 40 36 14. ⓐⓑⓒ pp.59, 61

Film producer Péby Guisez and his wife Corinne inherited this estate in 1987 and have since invested heavily in its success. The vineyards, split between ACs St-Émilion Grand Cru and Côtes de Castillon, have been improved and a new fermentation cellar built. The wines are full and concentrated, Ch. Faugères a little more structured than the Côtes de Castillon Ch. Cap de Faugères.

Château de Fieuzal

33850 Léognan. Tel 05 56 64 77 86; fax 05 56 64 18 88. ⓐⓑⓒ pp.34, 37

This estate was remodelled in the 1970s and 1980s and now makes some of the best wines in Pessac-Léognan AC. The reds are dense and firmly structured for long aging; the whites are lush and balanced with wonderful tropical fruit aromas in their youth. Second wine (red and white): l'Abeille de Fieuzal.

Château Figeac

33330 St-Émilion. Tel 05 57 24 72 26; fax 05 57 74 45 74. ⓐⓑ pp.56, 61

The vineyard at Ch. Figeac extends over an even greater percentage of the *graves anciennes* than Ch. Cheval-Blanc, hence the high percentage of Cabernet Sauvignon and Cabernet Franc (70 per cent) in the wines. This gives them a Médoc 'feel' when they are young, and the potential for long aging. Oak vats are still used to vinify part of the production and the grape skins are pressed in old hydraulic basket presses. The owner since 1947, Thierry Manoncourt, has been largely responsible for the continuing prestige of this Premier Grand Cru Classé. Second wine: la Grangeneuve de Figeac.

Château Fourcas-Dupré

33480 Listrac-Médoc. Tel 05 56 58 01 07; fax 05 56 58 02 27. ⓐⓑ pp.27, 29

Situated just north of the town of Listrac this estate produces firm, tannic wines that benefit from bottle age. Cabernet Sauvignon is the dominant grape variety providing the structure and power in riper vintages.

Château Haut-Bergey

33850 Léognan. Tel 05 56 64 05 22; fax 05 56 64 06 98. ⓐⓑⓒ pp. 34, 37

Since its purchase by Sylviane Garcin in 1991, this property in Pessac-Léognan AC has been totally restored: the 18th-century château has been renovated and a new barrel cellar and vathouse constructed. The wines have steadily progressed, so this is definitely an estate to keep an eye on in the future. The production is mainly red wine made from 70 per cent Cabernet Sauvignon and 30 per cent Merlot.

Château Haut-Brion

113 avenue Jean Jaurès, 33600 Pessac. Tel 05 56 00 29 30; fax 05 56 98 75 14. ⓐⓑⓒ pp.32, 37

Accorded Premier Cru status in the 1855 Classification, this was the only estate nominated for reds outside the Médoc. It has been owned by the American Dillon family since 1935. A high-tech *cuverie*, designed by manager Jean Delmas, was installed in 1991. The wine is deep and intense with subdued, layered fruit and fine but powerful tannic structure. There is also a tiny amount of white. Second wine: (red) Bahans-Haut-Brion.

Château Haut-Macô

33710 Tauriac. Tel 05 57 68 81 26; fax 05 57 68 91 97. ⓐⓑ pp. 67, 69

The vineyard of this property in the Côtes de Bourg has been steadily extended over the last 30 years. It covers a range of soils, which has inspired the planting of a greater proportion of Cabernet Sauvignon and Cabernet Franc than is usual here. This gives the wines a certain complexity in a ripe vintage. The modern, circular barrel cellar is worth a visit.

Château Kirwan

33460 Cantenac. Tel 05 57 88 71 00; fax 05 57 87 57 20. ⓐⓑ pp.26, 29

The majority of the vineyards of this Margaux Troisième Cru are located on the gravelly plateau of Cantenac. The château dates from the 18th century, rebuilt by the owner Mark Kirwan who comes from Galway in Ireland. After a rather indifferent period, the wines have recently regained their lustre, with the help of Michel Rolland, and are now full and aromatic with plenty of stylish oak. Second wine: les Charmes de Kirwan.

Château Labégorce-Zédé
33460 Soussans. Tel 05 57 88 71 31; fax 05 57 88 72 54. ⊘⦿ pp.26, 29
This small but dynamic estate in Margaux makes excellent wines that are rich, elegant and structured for aging. Much of the success is due to the astute management of Luc Thienpont whose family owns the estate. A generic Bordeaux, Z de Zédé, is made from grapes grown down on the *palus* near the Gironde. Second wine: Domaine Zédé.

Château Lafaurie-Peyraguey
33210 Bommes. Tel 05 56 95 53 09; fax 05 56 95 53 01. ⊘⦿ pp.42, 45
Since the sumptuous 1983 vintage this Sauternes Premier Cru has consistently produced some of the best wines in the AC. Rich and unctuous with tropical fruit flavours, these are truly great Sauternes. The unusual, square château has a medieval appearance and the tiny towers and gateway indeed date from the 13th century.

Château Lafite-Rothschild
33250 Pauillac. Tel 05 56 73 18 18; fax 05 56 59 26 83. ⊘⦿ pp.18, 21
This is a wine of great finesse as well as concentration. In the 18th century Lafite was owned by Alexandre, Marquis de Ségur who also owned Châteaux Latour and Calon-Ségur. It has been owned by the Rothschilds since 1868. The vineyard adjoins that of Mouton and there is a magnificent circular barrel cellar designed by Spanish architect Ricardo Bofill, where concerts are sometimes held. Second wine: les Carruades de Lafite.

Château Lagrange
33250 St-Julien Beychevelle. Tel 05 56 59 23 63; fax 05 56 59 26 09. ⊘⦿ pp.15, 21
Japanese owners Suntory have spent a considerable amount rebuilding this estate. The vineyard has been extended, a sophisticated vathouse and air-conditioned cellars built and the château restored. The wines are now spectacularly good and have

ripe fruit extract and a fine but firm tannic structure. Second wine: les Fiefs de Lagrange.

Château la Lagune
33290 Ludon. Tel 05 57 88 82 77; fax 05 57 88 82 70. ⊘⦿ pp.24, 29
The wines of this Haut-Médoc Troisième Cru are always deemed transitionary in style between those of the Médoc and Graves. They are mellow, elegant and overtly oaky in youth with good aging potential. The warm mesoclimate and sandy, pebbly soils of this zone help achieve good ripeness in the Cabernet Sauvignon grapes. The property has been owned by the Champagne house Ayala since 1961.

Château Lamothe-de-Haux
33550 Haux. Tel 05 56 23 05 07; fax 05 56 23 24 49. ⊘⦿⦿⦿ pp.49, 53
This estate in the Premières Côtes de Bordeaux takes its name from the acutely angled slope on which it is located, la Motte. The underground cellars are impressive and the wines are flavoursome and show the crisp red fruit expression of this AC.

Château de Landiras
33720 Landiras. Tel 05 56 62 44 70; fax 05 56 62 43 78. ⊘⦿⦿ pp.35, 37
Owner Peter Vinding-Diers helped pioneer the cleaner, fruitier style of white Graves back in the 1980s when working at Ch. Rahoul with Australian winemaker Brian Croser. Ch. de Landiras is his latest project, the vineyard reconstituted from virtually nothing. Principally white Graves are produced here from barrel-fermented Sémillon with a little Sauvignon Gris. The wines are crisp and fresh with an exotic cocktail of fruit aromas.

Peter Vinding-Diers also produces another good Graves, Domaine la Grave.

Château Lanessan
33460 Cussac Fort Médoc. Tel 05 56 58 94 80; fax 05 56 58 93 10. ⊘⦿ pp.27, 29
Visits to this estate in the Haut-Médoc include a tour of the equestrian museum, Musée du Cheval, as well as the cellars. The property is a large and rambling affair, grouped with two other estates owned by the same family. The wines, which have well-extracted fruit and a tannic edge, are traditional in style, and can be tasted and bought here.

Châteaux Langoa-Barton and Léoville-Barton
33250 St-Julien-Beychevelle. Tel 05 56 59 06 05; fax 05 56 59 14 29. ⊘⦿ pp.17, 21
These are two of the best-value Crus Classés in the Médoc. Purchased by Hugh Barton in the 19th century, Deuxième Cru Léoville and Troisième Cru Langoa are still owned by the Barton family today. The 18th-century residence belongs to Ch. Langoa, but the wine-making facilities are shared by the two estates. The wines are always full-bodied, the Léoville more powerful and structured. Second wine: Lady Langoa (produced from grapes from both estates).

Château Langoiran
33550 Langoiran. Tel 05 56 67 08 55; fax 05 56 67 32 87. ⊘⦿⦿⦿ pp.49, 53
The domaine is situated within the ramparts of the medieval château building, the ruins of which loom above. The cellars here have been modernized but a portion of them is located in the former prison chapel of the old castle. Ch. Langoiran is a simple, fruity, aromatic Prèmieres Côtes de Bordeaux, while the prestige Cuvée, Ch. Tour de Langoiran, is aged in oak barrels and is more concentrated and complex. The owners, Francis and Liliane Neeser, are welcoming hosts.

Château Latour
33250 Pauillac. Tel 05 56 73 19 80; fax 05 56 73 19 81. ⊘⏺
pp.17, 21
The characteristics of this great and wonderfully consistent wine include density of colour, reticent bouquet and a deep powerful structure that ensures great longevity. The quality is linked to the wonderful vineyard the core of which, known as l'Enclos, surrounds the rather obscure little château and distinctive tower. The history of Latour can be traced back to the 14th century and the prestige of its wines to the 16th. It is now in French hands following 30 years of English ownership. Second wine: les Forts de Latour (considered as good as a Deuxième Cru).

Château des Laurets
33570 Puisseguin. Tel 05 57 74 63 40; fax 05 57 74 65 34. ⊘⏺
pp.58, 61
Two wines are produced at this estate, a Puisseguin and a Montagne-St-Émilion. Both have good fruit expression and plenty of reserve. This is one of the largest estates in the Libournais, the vineyard lying in one single unit despite being split between the two ACs.

Château Léoville-Las-Cases
33250 St-Julien-Beychevelle. Tel 05 56 59 25 26; fax 05 56 59 18 33. ⊗⏺ pp.17, 21
Owner Michel Delon has steadily raised the quality of this Deuxième Cru to the level of the Premiers Crus. The vineyard now totals nearly 100ha, with 55ha in the famous walled-in clos adjacent to Ch. Latour. The wines have the structure and austerity of a Pauillac, yet a seductive quality of fruit that is the hallmark of St-Julien. Since 1986 only about 40 per cent of the production goes toward the

premium label. Second wine: Clos du Marquis.

Château Loudenne
33340 St-Yzans-de-Médoc. Tel 05 56 73 17 80; fax 05 56 09 02 87. ⊘⏺⏺⏺ pp.19, 21
Purchased by Walter and Alfred Gilbey in 1875 Château Loudenne retains a certain English charm in the far reaches of the northern Médoc. The tour includes an historical perspective of the estate in the Petit Pavillon as well as visits to the cellars, the Salle de Vignoble and a wine tasting. Lunch is possible if booked in advance. The red wine is a classic medium-weight Médoc and the white Bordeaux crisp and dry.

Château Loumède
33390 Blaye. Tel 05 57 42 16 39; fax 05 57 42 25 30. ⊘⏺
pp.67, 69
Simple family domaine on the outskirts of Blaye producing good-value Premières Côtes de Blaye largely from Merlot. The estate is run by brother and sister Yves and Jocelyne Raynaud who, since 1990, have gradually integrated more rigorous production methods including greater selection and barrel aging.

Château Lousteau-Vieil
33410 Ste-Croix-du-Mont. Tel 05 56 63 39 27; fax 05 56 63 11 82. ⊘⏺⏺ pp.43, 45
The vineyard is located at 118m (390ft), the highest point in the sweet wine commune of Ste-Croix-du-Mont. The wines are light in style but always aromatic due to the high proportion of Muscadelle in the blend.

Château la Louvière
33850 Léognan. Tel 05 56 64 75 87; fax 05 57 98 59 ⊘⏺⏺
pp.34, 37
The jewel in the crown of André Lurton's properties. The beautiful 18th-century château is a classified monument. Although the wines were not nominated in the 1959 Graves classification, they are now considered on a par with the existing Crus Classés. The elegant white wine is made principally from

Sauvignon Blanc and the red, which is firm and concentrated, from 65 per cent Cabernet Sauvignon, 30 per cent Merlot and a little Cabernet Franc and Petit Verdot. Second wine (red and white): L de la Louvière

Château Lynch-Bages
33250 Pauillac. Tel 05 56 73 24 00; fax 05 56 59 26 42. ⊘⏺⏺
pp.17, 21
This Cinquième Cru Pauillac normally commands the price of a Deuxième Cru. The wines are dark, rich and generous with lots of succulent fruit, making them attractive when young but with a structure for long aging. Owner Jean-Michel Cazes is a human dynamo who also oversees the AXA-Millésimes viticultural empire. Since 1990 a small amount of Blanc de Lynch-Bages has been produced at the estate. Second wine: Ch. Haut-Bages-Averous.

Château de Malle
33210 Preignac. Tel 05 56 62 36 86; fax 05 56 76 82 40. ⊘⏺⏺
pp.37, 40, 45
The château of Malle with its celebrated Italian gardens is registered as a historical monument in France and is well worth visiting. English-speaking visitors should make a prior appointment. This Deuxième Cru produces excellent wines – less powerful than some Sauternes but balanced and with a wonderful fruit character. The estate also produces a very good dry white Graves, M de Malle.

Château Malromé
33490 St-André du Bois. Tel 05 56 76 44 92; fax 05 56 76 45 29. ⊘⏺⏺ pp.50, 53
Once the family home and summer retreat of the celebrated French painter Henri de

Toulouse-Lautrec. The château, now a museum dedicated to the artist, can be visited by appointment. The estate also produces a fairly satisfying red Bordeaux Supérieur AC with a Belle Epoque label.

Château Margaux
33460 Margaux. Tel 05 57 88 83 83; fax 05 57 88 31 32. ⊘❶⊙ pp.24, 26, 29
This Premier Cru is presently at its apogee, with a string of successful vintages dating back to 1978. The wines are elegant and aromatic with deceptive power and concentration. The château and first year cellar date from the 19th century with the vaulted second year cellar added in 1982. A small cooperage produces 30 per cent of the oak barrels used. There is a rich but expensive dry white wine, Pavillon Blanc, made from 100 per cent Sauvignon Blanc. The second wine, Pavillon Rouge, is also extremely fine.

Château Maucaillou
33480 Moulis-en-Médoc. Tel 05 56 58 01 23; fax 05 56 58 00 88. ⊘❶ pp.27, 29
A visit here provides a well-rounded wine education. There is a wine museum and school as well as cellars to tour. The vineyard is located on the gravel hillock at Grand-Poujeaux alongside Châteaux Poujeaux and Chasse-Spleen. The wines are soft, supple and agreeable to drink at an early age.

Château Meyney
33180 St-Estèphe. Tel 05 56 95 53 00; fax 05 56 95 53 01. ⊘❶ pp.18, 21
A former priory, Ch. Meyney has a wonderful situation overlooking the Gironde estuary. The wines are of Cru Classé level, being rich, ripe and intense with a firm tannic structure. Second wine: Prieur de Meyney.

Château Montrose
33180 St-Estèphe. Tel 05 56 59 30 12; fax 05 56 59 38 48. ⊗❶ pp.18, 21
Classified as a Deuxième Cru, there are few wines that can

match Montrose for its strength and staying power. The estate overlooks the Gironde estuary just south of the village of St-Estèphe, and has been owned by the Charmolüe family since 1889. The wines, dominated by Cabernet Sauvignon, are firm, concentrated and vigorous. Along with those of Cos d'Estournel, they are, without doubt, the finest in St-Estèphe AC. Second wine: la Dame de Montrose.

Château Moulin-Pey-Labrie
33126 Fronsac. Tel 05 57 51 14 37; fax 05 57 51 53 45. ⊘❶ pp.66, 69
A well-sited hilltop vineyard located on the site of a ruined windmill. Owners Grégoire and Bénédicte Hubau produce superbly crafted wines that are rich, ripe and aromatic without any of the rusticity associated with the Canon-Fronsacs of yesteryear. They also produce a more supple Fronsac, Ch. Haut-Lariveau, made from 100 per cent Merlot.

Château Mouton-Rothschild
33250 Pauillac. Tel 05 56 73 21 29; fax 05 56 73 21 28. ⊘❶⊙ pp.18, 21
Promoted from Deuxième to Premier Cru in 1973, Mouton is a powerful, opulent wine made from a minimum 80 per cent Cabernet Sauvignon. The panache of this estate is derived from the zest of its late owner Baron Philippe de Rothschild who, amongst other things, initiated estate bottling in 1924 and the legendary labels painted by artists for each new vintage. The wine museum is included on the tour.

Château Nairac
33720 Barsac. Tel 05 56 27 16 16; fax 05 56 27 26 50. ⊘⊙ pp.43, 45
The vineyard and cellars date from 1610 but the actual château was built by a Huguenot négociant in 1786. Selective picking of only botrytized grapes and fermentation and maturation in new oak barrels produces a concentrated, oaky style of

Barsac best consumed after ten years' bottle age.

Château Palmer
33460 Margaux. Tel 05 57 88 72 72; fax 05 57 88 37 16. ⊘❶ pp.26, 29
One of the most consistent estates in the Médoc, the wines, supple and elegant, selling for more than the Troisième Cru status would indicate. Established by the English General Charles Palmer in the early 19th century, the château was built in 1856. A high-tech vatroom was installed in 1995. Second wine: Réserve du Général.

Château Pape-Clément
216 avenue de Dr. Nancel Pénard, 33600 Pessac. Tel 05 56 07 04 11; fax 05 56 07 36 70. ⊘⊘❶⊙ pp.33, 37
The origins of this Graves Cru Classé can be traced back to 1305 – the owner, Bertrand de Goth, later Pope Clément V. The wines have been back on form since the 1986 vintage, the reds ripe, velvety and powerful, but needing time, and the whites increasingly rich and aromatic. Second wine: (red) le Clémentin.

Château Pavie
33330 St-Émilion. Tel 05 57 55 43 43; fax 05 57 24 63 99. ⊘❶ pp.59, 61
This is the second largest, after Ch. Figeac, of St-Émilion's Premiers Grands Crus Classés. The vineyard is wonderfully situated on a south-facing slope just outside the town, and the cellars, hewn out of the side of

the slope, date from the 12th century. The wines are supple, aromatic and remarkably attractive when young, although they have the potential to age.

Château Pétrus
33500 Pomerol. Tel 05 57 51 78 96; fax 05 57 51 79 79. ⊗⊕ pp.65, 69
Powerful, rich, layered and unctuous, Pétrus is a monumental wine and the most famous name in Pomerol. The demand for Pétrus has also given it the reputation for being one of the most expensive red wines in the world. Made almost entirely from Merlot grown on a 'buttonhole' of clay, it needs at least a dozen years in bottle to be at its best. There is little to see, just the vineyard and *cuverie*.

Château Pichon-Longueville
33250 Pauillac. Tel 05 56 73 17 17; fax 05 56 73 17 28. ⊘⊕ pp.17, 21
Since being purchased by AXA-Millésimes in 1987 and managed by Jean-Michel Cazes (Lynch-Bages), the wines of this Deuxième Cru have been on top form. The fairy-tale turreted château has been renovated and a state-of-the-art winery built. Second wine: les Tourelles de Longueville.

Château Pichon-Longueville-Comtesse-de-Lalande
33250 Pauillac. Tel 05 56 59 19 40; fax 05 56 59 29 78. ⊘⊕ pp.17, 21
The château looks out across the vineyards of Latour toward the Gironde. As at neighbouring Pichon-Longueville, the cellars and *cuverie* have been renovated. The wine is supple and elegant, perhaps due to the high percentage of Merlot in the blend, but can age for a good 15-20 years. Second wine: Réserve de la Comtesse.

Château Poujeaux
33480 Moulis-en-Médoc. Tel 05 56 58 02 96; fax 05 56 58 01 25. ⊘⊕ pp.27, 29
Located on the gravel outcrop in Moulis, this is another property that could argue for inclusion in

a revised 1855 Classification. The wines are both elegant and concentrated and include 40 per cent Merlot, a high percentage for the Médoc. A limited list of vintages is sold at the property and there is an interesting tasting case of each of the 4 principal grape varieties, together with their blended version. Second wine: la Salle de Poujeaux.

Château Prieuré-Lichine
33460 Cantenac. Tel 05 57 88 36 28; fax 05 57 88 78 93. ⊘⊕ pp.26, 29
A former Benedictine priory, the château is open to visitors all year round. The property was purchased by Alexis Lichine in 1951, and he painstakingly extended the vineyard from 11ha to the present 69ha by bartering and exchanging parcels of land throughout the communes of Arsac, Labarde, Cantenac, Margaux and Soussans. His son Sacha now owns and manages the estate, with Michel Rolland as the consultant enologist. The wines are ripe, elegant and aromatic. Second wine: Château de Clairefont.

Les Producteurs Réunis
Puisseguin, 33570 Lussac. Tel 05 57 55 50 40; fax 05 57 74 57 43. ⊘⊕ pp.58, 61
This co-operative in Puisseguin accounts for 45 per cent of the production of Lussac-St-Émilion and 35 per cent of Puisseguin-St-Émilion. A range of wines is available, including the regular Cuvée, Roc de Puisseguin (Roc de Lussac), and the top of the range for both ACs, Cuvée Renaissance, made from older vines and aged in oak barrels.

Château Puy-Bardens
33880 Cambes. Tel 05 56 21 31 14; fax 05 56 21 86 40. ⊘⊕⊕ pp.49, 53
This is one of the top producers in the lively Premières Côtes de Bordeaux AC. The tiny castle is perched on a hillock with an imposing view of the Garonne valley and the Graves AC. The wines are rich, textured and elegant and tastings take place in a friendly environment.

Château Puygueraud
33570 St-Cibard. Tel 05 57 40 61 04; fax 05 57 40 66 08. ⊘⊕ pp.58, 61
The flagship estate for the tiny Bordeaux-Côtes de Francs AC. Owned since 1946 by George Thienpont, the vineyard was replanted only in the latter part of the 1970s. The wines, made from a Merlot-Cabernet blend, are tannic, robust and complex with a good potential for aging and are very good value.

Château Rauzan-Ségla
33460 Margaux. Tel 05 57 88 82 10; fax 05 57 88 34 54. ⊘⊕ pp.26, 29
Already improved since 1983, its purchase by Chanel in 1994 has turned this Margaux Deuxième Cru upside down in the quest for its former glory. The vineyard has been replanted and drains laid, the buildings renovated, new equipment installed and the percentage of new oak barrels increased. Recent vintages have shown its potential, having soft ripe fruit, seductive bouquet and great concentration. The spelling with a Z was introduced in 1994. Second wine: Ségla.

Château Raymond-Lafon
33210 Sauternes. Tel 05 56 63 21 02; fax 05 56 63 19 58. ⊘⊕ p.42
Originally created in 1850, too late to be placed in the 1855 Classification; today the wines are the equal of the top Crus Classés and command the same prices. It was bought in 1972 by Pierre Meslier, the former manager at Ch. d'Yquem. The vineyard lies close to that of Yquem and the wines are made with the same care.

Château Rieussec
33210 Fargues-de-Langon. Tel 05 56 62 20 71; fax 05 56 76 27 82. ⊘⊕ pp.41, 45

Situated on a hill adjacent to Ch. d'Yquem, this domaine has the reputation for producing intensely sweet Sauternes. It has been owned since 1984 by Lafite-Rothschild who have steadily introduced more modern equipment and a greater percentage of new oak barrels.

Château la Rivière
33126 la Rivière. Tel 05 57 55 56 56; fax 05 57 24 94 39. ⊘⦿ pp.67, 69
The most majestic property in Fronsac AC, with a turreted Renaissance château, extensive parkland, a sweeping view over the Dordogne, and 5ha of cellars quarried from the limestone bedrock. The new proprietor has dispensed with the stock of older vintages and brought in Michel Rolland as consultant. The wines, which hitherto have been vigorous but rather hard-edged, look set to change in style.

Château St-Georges
St-Georges-de-Montagne, 33570 Montagne. Tel 05 57 74 62 11; fax 05 57 74 58 62. ⊘⦿ pp.58, 61
The Louis XVI château stands strikingly on the crest of a hill just to the north of St-Émilion. Located in the satellite AC St-Georges-St-Émilion, the south-facing vineyards of Ch. St-Georges are better sited than many in the St-Émilion AC itself. The wines are rich and concentrated and, although variable of late, can sometimes be better than many St-Émilion Grands Crus.

Château de Sales
33500 Libourne. Tel 05 57 51 04 92; fax 05 57 25 23 91. ⊘⦿ pp.65, 69
The property has been owned by the de Lambert family since 1490 and is the largest in Pomerol

with 47.5ha and an imposing château – the complete antithesis of the normally tiny, unobtrusive Pomerol estate. The vineyard is situated on the sandier soils to the north-west of the AC and, consequently, the wines are lighter and less opulent than those produced on Pomerol's high plateau. They are, however, supple, fruity, consistent in quality and reasonably priced.

Château Smith-Haut-Lafitte
33650 Martillac. Tel 05 56 30 72 30; fax 05 56 30 96 26. ⊘⦿⦿ pp.35, 37
A veritable revolution has taken place at this ancient property in Pessac-Léognan since it was acquired by Daniel and Florence Cathiard in 1990. The 18th-century Chartreuse has been renovated, the vineyards restored, wine-making facilities modernized, new reception room and barrel cellar constructed and a cooperage installed. The whites are made from 100 per cent Sauvignon and are concentrated and aromatic. The reds, as of the 1994 vintage, are superbly concentrated. Second wine: les Hauts de Smith.

Château Sociando-Mallet
33180 St-Seurin de Cadourne. Tel 05 56 59 36 57; fax 05 56 59 70 88. ⊘⦿ pp.18, 29
This 'super' Cru Bourgeois in the Haut-Médoc would definitely warrant a place in a revised version of the 1855 Classification. The vineyard has the well-drained gravel soils found at the great estates in Pauillac and St-Estèphe, allowing Cabernet Sauvignon to ripen fully and produce fine, complex, textured wines that are structured and ageworthy. Second wine: la Demoiselle de Sociando-Mallet.

Château Soutard
33330 St-Émilion. Tel 05 57 24 72 23; fax 05 57 24 66 94. ⊘⦿ pp.58, 61
One of the most impressive properties in St-Émilion, located on the northern extreme of the limestone plateau. The wines are 'classical' St-Émilions – robust, dense and powerful, with a capacity for long aging. François de Ligneris, one of the younger generation of winemakers in St-Émilion and manager of this family estate, is usually happy to take the time to explain the terroir and wine-making methods at Ch. Soutard as well as its environmentally conscious approach to viticulture.

Château Suduiraut
33210 Preignac. Tel 05 56 63 27 29; fax 05 56 63 07 00. ⊘⦿ pp.41, 45
This Premier Cru Sauternes is now owned by insurance company AXA-Millésimes and is undergoing extensive renovation. It will consequently be closed to the public until 1998. The estate comprises one unbroken unit of vineyard, woodland and 17th-century château with gardens designed by le Nôtre. Ch. Suduiraut at its best (1989, 90) is a superb wine, rich, textured and honeyed with the aroma of exotic fruits, but can be variable in quality. The new ownership is sure to add greater consistency.

Château Tayac
33710 St-Seurin-de-Bourg. Tel 05 57 68 40 60; fax 05 57 68 29 93. ⊘⦿⦿⦿ pp.67, 69
This domaine has a wealth of history and wine-making prowess as well as a superb position overlooking the Gironde. The Renaissance-style château dates from the 19th century but the English presence here in the Middle Ages is attested to by the watchtower built around 1356 under the orders of the Black Prince. The Cocks et Féret edition of 1868 listed Tayac as a 'Premier Cru Bourgeois du Bourgeois' and today it is still one of the best estates in the Côtes de Bourg.

The top-of-the-range le Prestige is made largely from Cabernet Sauvignon.

Château Thieuley

33670 la Sauve-Majeure. Tel 05 56 23 00 01; fax 05 56 23 34 37. ✅⚬◉⚑ pp.51, 53
An impeccably run estate in the Entre-Deux-Mers, Ch. Thieuley has the pristine apprearance of a Cru Classé in the Médoc. Francis Courselle was one of the first to install modern systems of vinification in the region and consequently to produce fresh, aromatic white wines. Apart from the classic white Bordeaux, there is a barrel-fermented version, Cuvée Francis Courselle.

Château la Tour-Blanche

33210 Bommes. Tel 05 57 98 02 73; fax 05 57 98 02 78. ✅⚬ pp.42, 45
This Sauternes Premier Cru has been owned by the French Ministry of Agriculture since 1911. The wines had for a long time been of little interest until the 1988 vintage, when investment and a change in methods of vinification began to pay dividends. New oak barrels are now used for fermentation and maturation and the wines have the rich unctuousness of the great Sauternes.

Château la Tour-de-By

33340 Bégadan. Tel 05 56 41 51 53; fax 05 56 41 38 72. ✅⚬ pp.19, 21
This large estate in Médoc AC takes its name from the old stone lighthouse that stands in the vineyards overlooking the Gironde. Co-owner and manager Marc Pagès has ensured a wonderful consistency in the wines over the years and it is rare that they disappoint. Vigorous with good fruit extract and tannic structure, the wines provide excellent drinking after 5–6 years' bottle age.

Château Tour Haut-Caussan

33340 Blaignan. Tel 05 56 09 00 77; fax 05 56 09 06 24. ✅⚬ pp.19, 21
Beautifully polished wines are produced at this estate, which is run on semi-organic lines. The ripeness of the Merlot and Cabernet fruit and the complexity, and finesse produced by the high percentage of new oak barrels, puts them amongst the best in Médoc AC. The vineyard at Caussan surrounds an 18th-century windmill restored by owner Philippe Courrian.

Château Tour-du-Haut-Moulin

33460 Cussac Fort Médoc. Tel 05 56 58 91 10; fax 05 56 58 99 30. ✅⚬ pp.26, 29
The wines at this Haut-Médoc estate, run by brother and sister Lionel and Béatrice Poitou, are rarely disappointing and represent good value for money. There is a small tasting room and older vintages are usually available for purchase.

Château le Tuquet

33640 Beautiran. Tel 05 56 20 21 23; fax 05 56 20 21 83. ✅◉⚬ pp.35, 37
A large domaine producing well-constituted red and white Graves. The tiny Chartreuse was designed by the architect Victor Louis in the 18th century. The cellars and outbuildings date from the same period.

Union des Producteurs de Rauzan

33420 Rauzan. Tel 05 57 84 13 22; fax 05 57 84 12 67. ✅◉⚬⚑ pp.50, 53
As well as being the largest wine producer in the Gironde, the Rauzan co-operative is also the largest producer of AC wines in France. Situated near the medieval English fortress of Rauzan, it is now a high-tech operation with modern equipment and approach. There is a shop for tastings and sales with a number of labels available, including the fairly consistent Comte de Rudel Entre-Deux-Mers and Bordeaux Supérieur.

Vieux-Château-Certan

33500 Pomerol. Tel 05 57 51 17 33; fax 05 57 25 35 08. ✅⚬ pp.64, 69
A neighbour of Pétrus, this domaine produces one of the most elegant wines in Pomerol. The vineyard has a high proportion of the same *graves anciennes* found at Châteaux Figeac and Cheval-Blanc, just across the way in St-Émilion – hence the high percentage (for Pomerol) of Cabernet Franc and Cabernet Sauvignon (up to 45 per cent) used in the blend. The wines are consequently deeply coloured, rich and plump with a refined tannic structure.

Vieux-Château-Gaubert

33640 Portets. Tel 05 56 67 04 32; fax 05 56 67 52 76. ✅◉⚬ pp.35, 37
The listed 18th-century château still has to be restored but priority has been given to the vineyards and the wines since Dominique Haverlan purchased the property in 1988. The white wine is a barrel-fermented, delicately aromatic Graves; the red is dry and firm.

Château d'Yquem

33210 Sauternes. Tel 05 57 98 07 07; fax 05 57 98 07 08. ✖⚬ pp.41, 42, 45
The property of the Lur-Saluces family since 1785, Ch. d'Yquem was distinguished as Premier Cru Supérieur in the 1855 Classification, and is still recognized as the greatest sweet wine in the world. It is difficult to visit and the château, which was constructed around a 15th-century fortified farmhouse, is always off limits. The wine is made with minute attention to detail. Only nobly rotted grapes are picked, giving a yield the equivalent of one glass of wine per vine. The juice is fermented in 100 per cent new oak barrels and matured there for three and a half years. The wines are rich, powerful and extremely long-lived.

Index of Other Wine Producers

For Main Wine Producers see pages 70–79.

Picture Credits All photographs Cephas Picture Library. Photographer Mick Rock, except Nigel Blythe 1, 4, 10, 43, 45, 50, 60, 61, 68; Rosine Mazin 48.

Publisher's Acknowledgments Trevor Lawrence (map illustrations), Aziz Khan (grape artworks), Steven Marwood (bottle photography).